Wheel and Tire
Performance Handbook

Wheel and Tire
Performance Handbook

Richard Newton

MOTORBOOKS

First published in 2007 by Motorbooks, an imprint of
MBI Publishing Company LLC, Galtier Plaza, Suite 200,
380 Jackson Street, St. Paul, MN 55101 USA

Motorbooks titles are also available at discounts in bulk
quantity for industrial or sales-promotional use. For details
write to Special Sales Manager at MBI Publishing Company,
Galtier Plaza, Suite 200, 380 Jackson Street, St. Paul, MN
55101 USA.

To find out more about our books, join us online at
www.motorbooks.com.

ISBN-13: 978-0-7603-3144-6

Editor: Jennifer Bennett
Designer: Chris Fayers

Printed in China

On the cover: A big, bad turbocharged Porsche needs big,
bad tires to get its power to the ground. *Richard Newton*

On the back cover: The huge voids in this tire's tread make
it effective in mud. On the other hand, there's very little
tread to come into contact with a hard-surfaced road. This
tire could make for very exciting times on wet pavement.
Richard Newton

About the author
Richard Newton is an ASE-certified Master Technician who
spent 15 years in the automotive service industry before
becoming an automotive magazine editor and freelance
writer. He has written five books to date, including *Corvette
C5 Performance Projects*, *Ultimate Garage Handbook*, and
Autocross Performance Handbook. He currently resides in
Bonita Springs, Florida.

CONTENTS

CHAPTER 1
VEHICLE DYNAMICS

Tires aren't just important, they're the whole deal. The only contact your car has with the road is the rubber on your tires. No matter how much power you put out, or what sort of suspension you have on your car, it all comes down to four little patches of rubber. That's why the major goal is to keep all four tires on the ground all of the time.

There may be a few reasons why you care about tires. First, you believe your tires and wheels make a statement about who you are. Your tires and wheels tell the world about you. Your low profile tires and 20-inch rims give you street cred. They make a statement without you opening your mouth.

Then there is the restoration crowd. They want the world to know that they care enough to have a perfectly restored car. When they drive down the road they want everything to be just like it was decades ago. They want the same road feel, and they want people to appreciate what cars were like back then. This group makes a statement about the value of the past.

There's still another group of folks who want their cars to perform at their highest level. They want the world to know that their vehicles are fast and that they have the ability to drive fast. Even more important, they let their tires and wheels announce this performance to the whole world.

Actually, these groups are all blended together for one common goal. You really can't have high-performance tires and wheels and look dorky. Likewise you can't put cheap wheels and tires on your car and expect to go fast. It's never a question of one thing or another. It's really a question of which side you want to emphasize.

Tires and wheels combine to make a very strong visual statement. Here's a Fuchs forged wheel with an RSR finish. This is on a 1973 Porsche 911S. Even the interior of the fender is finished correctly.

*Left: Another Porsche, but an earlier car with a steel chrome wheel. The cost of chroming these wheels will be more than the cost of new alloy wheels. Then again, an alloy wheel on a 356 Porsche just wouldn't be right. **Right:** Porsche used some unique wheels in the early cars. Okay, they really used a variation of the VW wheel. The suitcase shown here was a factory option.*

FIVE CONCEPTS OF HANDLING

One of the most misused and least understood concepts is handling. All you have to do is visit any Internet forum and people will be complaining, or bragging, about their car's handling. Usually they never state what they actually mean. It's usually something to the effect of "My car really handles since I did [XYZ]."

I'm going to break down handling into five basic items. Each component is a part of the total package. The whole secret here is to be able to utilize all of your tire's performance. So little rubber actually comes into contact with the pavement at one time that we have to optimize each and every aspect of what we call handling.

Five Basic Concepts

1. Response – The *time* between input to output
2. Precision – The *consistency* of output from a fixed input
3. Gain – The *amount* of output from a given input
4. Progression – The *consistency* of the gain
5. Balance – Bias toward oversteer and understeer

Response

A good car should respond to your inputs. When you ask the car to do something it should follow your commands, and it should react almost instantly. On a street driven car you should feel as if you're connected to the car. When you turn the steering wheel, the car should turn. Is there a lag between the time when you turn the wheel and when the car actually starts to turn? A huge part of the handling equation is having a responsive car.

Precision

Does the car do what you want it to do, or do you have to keep making corrections to get the car to maintain the desired line? How much effort is necessary to maintain a given line? Do you have to make a series of mini corrections, or can you maintain the line easily? How much precision does your car have?

Gain

Gain means that you have a constant rate of turning relative to how much you're turning the steering wheel. If you hold the steering wheel steady does the car track on the desired driving line or do you have to make corrections? With a fixed steering input does the car turn a little or a lot?

Progression

Progression means that there is proportionality to the way the car reacts to driver inputs. If you make a quarter turn on the steering wheel and the car turns 10 degrees, then a half turn of the steering wheel should result in a 20 degree turning angle. There has to be a relationship between what you do and what the car actually does. You want this relationship to be constant.

On some cars, for example, a little bit of steering produces almost no turning. Then when you turn the steering wheel a little more the car starts to turn really quickly. This would be an example of a car with steering that is non-linear.

Increasing steering input in some cars produces very little change in steering while increasing the steering input in other vehicles may even *reduce* cornering power. Both of these examples are non-progressive, but the second case is even less progressive. In other words, increasing the amount of turning at the steering wheel the car actually turns less.

The goal is to have a car that responds to your inputs in a progressive manner. You don't want, or need, any big surprises. You want a steady progressive response from your car or truck.

In the middle 1960s, tire companies began reducing the height of the sidewall. This gave cars such as the Mustang a sportier look. No one at the time envisioned where this trend would end up.

Balance

Is the car balanced? Does the tail of the car lose adhesion before the front? Does the nose of the car want to push towards the outside of the turn? Are both ends of the car working at an optimum point?

Oversteer and understeer are vital to understanding the way a car corners. It's really about which end of the car runs out of adhesion first. In an understeer situation the front tires break free first, wanting to go to the outside of the turn. In an oversteer condition, the back end of the car loses adhesion first and goes to the outside of the turn.

An unbalanced car often feels unpredictable and unstable to a driver. When you drive hard into a corner you need to have confidence that you'll come out of that corner with no surprises. You need all four tires working at their maximum. It does very little good to have the front tires stick and the rear tires slide out from under you.

Keep in mind that the tire with the least traction is going to set your cornering limit. It does no good to have wonderful traction at the front of your car if the rear tires lack traction. This works the same way in reverse. If you lack adhesion on the front tires you're not going to be able to hold the car in a turn. Forward bite just doesn't matter if you can't make the turn.

FUNDAMENTALS OF TRACTION

Tires are all about traction. But, traction is one of the most misunderstood components of tires, and of driving. Traction is really the friction of the tire against the road. Two critical items are involved.

First is the ability of the rubber in the tire to interact with the pavement. That's all about the rubber compound in the tire. Soft rubber is going to grip the pavement better than a hard rubber compound. The problem is we want the rubber to last a certain amount of time.

A fine line exists between optimal adhesion and having the rubber last for a given period of time. In NASCAR that time may only be 50 laps, while you might expect the tires on your SUV to last over 30,000 miles. At what point do you sacrifice adhesion for wear?

The second factor in traction is how much of your tire actually touches the pavement at any given time. Obviously, the greater the area of the contact between your tire and the pavement, the more traction you're going to have. The goal is to have as much contact as possible.

One of the great myths is that a larger tire will give you more contact with the pavement. Wrong. The contact area of your tire is a function of the weight of the car, and the amount of air in your tires. It has absolutely nothing to do

continued on page 12

Left: This is a Corvette that has everything. Not only does it have the correct reproduction tires, but the wheel color is correct as well. These Corvette wheel covers, or hubcaps, are polished with a chrome spinner bolted to the center. *Right:* When your car has no fenders it's essential that you have the correct wheels and tires. All of that rubber is on public display. This is a conservative approach with a fairly narrow white letter tire. Note how big the wheel weight is at the bottom of the wheel. That's a lot of weight. It's not a problem but it shows that the wheel and tire combination has a real heavy spot someplace.

This is the front wheel of the same car. Here you'll notice that the tire and wheel use a lot less weight for balancing.

Left: This is the sort of wheel that can consume your entire weekend. There's a point where wire wheels just get too hard to clean. It's also a major job to keep this type of wheel running true. Very few companies can rebuild a wire wheel correctly. Getting a wire wheel round is a very time-consuming operation. Plus, it takes years of experience to develop the necessary skill. *Right:* Ferrari has always done a wonderful job with wheels. This is a factory alloy wheel.

Now this is a very serious wheel. This is a center-lock front wheel on a Ferrari 512, a former Le Mans car. The trick with these old race cars is to get the tire dimensions correct. Keep in mind that these Avon slicks grip far better than anything that was used on the original cars. That means if you run this car seriously, you need to check the suspension connections on a regular basis.

continued from page 9

with the size of your tire. You can put really huge tires on your car but you won't necessarily get any more rubber coming into contact with the pavement. It's all about physics. How much weight is pushing the tire onto the ground? How much air is holding your car up?

The one thing a larger tire will do though is change the *shape* of the contact area between your tire and the pavement. The total area of the contact patch will remain the same as it was with the smaller tires, but the shape will change. That can be a good thing. Basically, traction or adhesion depends on three items.

- Compound Deformation
- Percent of Slip
- Footprint Shape

Compound Deformation

One way to get deformation is to use a lower tire pressure, which increases the footprint area that comes into contact with the road. Remember that there is no direct relationship between the size of the tire and the size of the footprint. The contact area is determined by load divided by tire pressure:

$$Load/psi = Contact\ Area$$

Since the weight of your car will remain constant (for the most part), changing the psi is the only way to change the size of the contact area. Now couple that fact with the notion that the tire can be designed to react differently to stress. A tire with what is called a low modulus will deform much more than a tire with a high modulus. A low modulus, or stiffness, allows much greater deformation and a larger contact patch.

The problem is that a tire with relatively low stiffness will need a greater inflation pressure. That increased tire pressure will reduce the effective size of the contact patch. It's just one giant balancing act with tires.

Percent of Slip

The slip angle is the angle between the direction in which a tire is aimed or steered and the actual direction of tire travel. The ideal here is to have 10 percent slip. In other words, for maximum grip a tire should be slipping about 10 percent. This slip is usually the same whether we're talking about part of the contact area, or the entire contact area.

Some race teams feel that when you go over 10 percent slip you're really out of control. If you're at less than 10 percent, you're not maximizing the car's forward motion. The best lap times will be when you're on that 10 percent knife-edge. Since the tire has only so much potential friction you need to optimize every bit of that friction.

Footprint Shape

The footprint, or contact patch shape is the part of the tire that touches the road. On tall tires, the contact patch is longer than wide. On short tires the opposite is true. The length-to-width ratio of this footprint will affect steering and cornering behavior. As a general rule of thumb, a larger center area will enhance straight-line stability and response time. A larger shoulder area will improve cornering performance. The key point here is that the shape of the contact patch is critical to handling.

TIRE DYNAMICS

The performance of your tires is really dependent on four basic vehicle issues. These are essentially tuning issues and are things that you can do to improve the combination of car and tire. The goal is to have the suspension work to keep as much rubber as possible in contact with the pavement.

Compliance
Load Distribution
Footprint Shape
Slip

Compliance

The basic definition of compliance is that something is yielding, or pliant. When it comes to the springs on your car it means softer, or more yielding. The more compliant

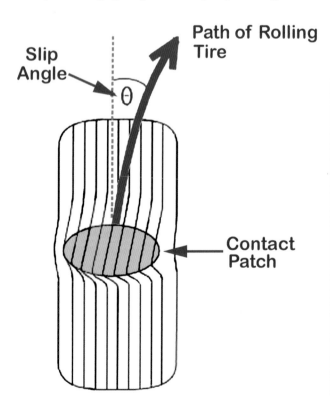

Slip Angle

Path of Rolling Tire

θ

Contact Patch

Race cars seem to have transitioned from the three-piece wheels to the single piece forged alloy wheel. OZ makes some of the strongest—and most expensive—wheels in the world. One thing to note here is that the wheel uses a center-mount system. More important, notice how little weight it took to balance this assembly. You can see the weight on the right side of the wheel directly behind the area where the spokes meet the rim.

Left: The front tires here are 345/40ZR/19. If you have to ask how much they cost, you shouldn't own this Ferrari. **Right:** This is a Lexus wheel that seems overly fussy. Wheels like this are hard to keep clean. The interesting thing is that only a few years ago a tire with this low of a profile would have been found only on a performance car. Now you can find them on cars that only go to the mall.

Left: *Nothing says retro rod like a wide white wall. This is a reproduction of a BFGoodrich Silvertown. A tire/wheel combination such as this is going to be a lot cheaper than an alloy wheel.* **Right:** *This painted wheel and the reproduction Firestone makes a tremendous statement. It's not necessary to spend a lot of money on tires and wheels. Just do it right and you can have stunning looks on a budget. This was the way this car left the Pontiac dealership over 40 years ago.*

Left: *The 1984 Corvette set the standards for big rubber—the car was actually designed around these tires. Originally the base wheels were going to be 15-inch steel. At the last minute they made the 16-inch alloy wheel the standard wheel. In retrospect that was a brilliant decision.* **Right:** *Wire wheels have an elegance that just can't be matched. The reproduction whitewall just adds to the whole statement.*

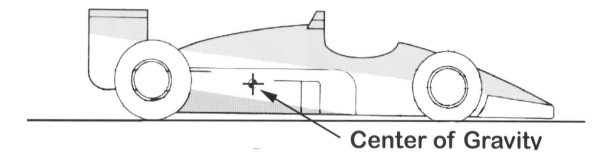

Center of Gravity

the total spring rate of the car, the more time the tire spends on the ground. You need to have tires on the ground to have traction. This is a very simple concept that seems to get lost at times.

Another important point is that compliance isn't just about the springs. It's about the total suspension system. The total package includes the springs as well as the shocks, sway bars, chassis, and tires. The goal is to keep the tires in contact with the pavement as much as possible.

One place you really don't want compliance though is in the chassis. You want your chassis as stiff as possible. A major role of the roll cage in modern cars is to take all of the compliance out of the chassis. Make the chassis of the car as stiff as possible and you've eliminated a variable in the handling equation. Chassis flex will make all the other tunable suspension control mechanisms insensitive or inoperative. You absolutely have to control the flex of the chassis for the other components to work properly.

Load Distribution

Three basic factors effect load distribution.

Center of gravity (Cg)
Roll center
Springs, sway bars, and shock absorbers

Center of Gravity: The center of gravity (Cg) is the point of perfect balance. The lower you can place the center of gravity the better, because a high center of gravity means more roll and less cornering power. Even more important is the simple fact that a lower center of gravity improves load distribution on the tires.

Let's look at this example:

Track width = 2 meters
Cg Height = .5 meter
Static load per tire 300 Kg @ 1.0 g
Outside Tire Load = 450 Kg
Inside Tire Load = *150 Kg*

Track width = 2 meters
Cg Height = .4 meter
Static load per tire 300 Kg @ 1.0 g
Outside Tire Load = 420 Kg
Inside Tire Load = *180 Kg*

Simply lowering the center of gravity places a much greater load on the inside tire when cornering. This is why when people lower their cars they say they improved the handling. Increasing the load on the inside tire enlarged the contact patch. Remember also that weight is a key factor in the size of the contact patch. More weight on a tire means a larger contact patch.

Roll Center: The roll center of a vehicle is the point, or axis, around which the vehicle rolls while cornering. This is an important concept since the force of the tire acts through this roll center. When your car is in a turn, centrifugal force causes the body of the car to lean toward the outside of the turn. This is called roll. This roll compresses the springs on the outside of the turn and allows the springs on the inside to extend.

When you view the car in a turn, it's apparent that the body is no longer horizontal to the road. The roll center is a theoretical point determined by the pivot point location and angles of the suspension linkages, about which the particular end of the vehicle rolls. A car has two roll centers when cornering: one generated by the suspension at each

continued on page 18

Every car has two roll centers, a roll center (RC) for the front and one for the rear. In almost every case, the rear RC will be higher than the front.

Left: *All-season tires are just fine for all around use. They usually wear well and do a nice job of getting you through the rain and winter slush.* **Above:** *Racing tire sidewalls have become virtual billboards. Michelin has even developed these appliqués rather than just painting their name on the sidewalls.* **Below:** *You thought the shock absorber had to be in a vertical position? These shocks cost more than your first home. Keep in mind though that the shock absorber is a major key to proper handling. That's why race teams spend the Gross National Product of a small nation to get the optimal shock.*

Left: These grooves are all about rain. The idea is that as the car goes down the road the water is captured in the grooves and thrown away from the tire's footprint. Keep in mind that aquaplaning (also called hydroplaning) is nothing more than having the tire lose contact with the pavement. These grooves are designed to prevent that. **Below:** In order for a tire to work properly it has to be attached to a stable platform. All of this tubing is just an attempt to stiffen the chassis. With very limited chassis flex this Viper can use the tires properly. **Bottom:** This is really a very basic suspension. It has upper and lower control arms. The big difference here is that the springs and shocks are mounted on top of the car and they operate via a long rod. The key thing here is that every item is very lightweight and adjustable.

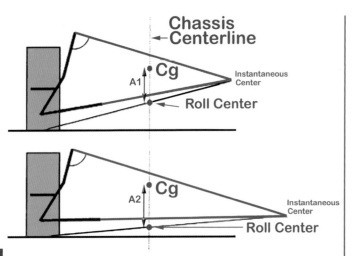

When you lower your car you lower the center of gravity. That's usually a good thing. The problem is that you also lower the roll center, which may not be a good thing. Notice in this example how lowering the Cg of the car dramatically changed the RC, and also the distance between the roll center and the Cg. Your car, and handling, is a series of connected variables. Every time you change one thing, five others are also changed.

continued from page 15

end of the car, and another that moves around as the car corners, brakes, accelerates, and does any combination of the former.

When you're cornering, your car will roll about this roll axis. The relationship between the height of the center of gravity and roll axis determines how much body roll takes place during cornering. The greater distance between the height of the center of gravity and the roll axis, the greater the body roll angle with a given lateral acceleration.

One important point to keep in mind is that most current cars are designed with fairly high roll centers. That means you need less spring force and less sway bar force to control body roll.

Springs: The springs, just like the sway bars and shocks, are used to tune suspension compliance. Remember that weight transfer causes body motion. Body motion is an effect of weight transfer, not the cause. The purpose of changing the springs, sway bars, and shocks is to *selectively* stiffen the suspension at a particular time, or under certain conditions, to reduce the grip of a given tire. The goal is to get better overall total balance.

There is generally a given sequence for making any changes to your car. You should start with the springs. The primary purpose of the springs on your vehicle is to keep the chassis from dragging on the pavement. Improved handling comes from getting the center of gravity as low as possible. You want the mass of your car as low as possible without making contact with the pavement. Soft springs help you attain this low Cg.

If you're really into extreme handling, such as in a race car, you want the spring's rate as low as possible. In other words, softer springs are better—if all of the other issues are properly sorted out. You don't want springs so stiff that the tires bounce off the pavement.

Another function of the springs is to damp out front-to-rear pitch. Your car shouldn't be acting like a see saw at the playground. If the springs don't damp chassis motion, then the shocks are going to have to do that job. That's not an ideal situation, since it requires excessive shock force.

One point to consider is if you're going to modify your chassis, the springs are where you should start. Most people start with shocks since they're easy to replace. That is just so wrong. Start with the springs, and remember stiffer is not always better. A lot of race engineers feel a race car should actually touch the track at some point during a really fast lap. They even put skid plates under the car for this purpose.

Also, don't forget that the tire is a spring. When people say that go karts have no springs they're technically wrong.

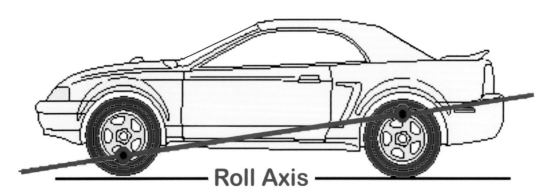

The roll axis of a car can be found by drawing a line that connects the front and rear roll centers. A roll axis that points down toward the front of the car is an understeering roll axis, and it is often found on high-performance cars

At one point this was a Sports Car Club of America (SCCA) Trans Am Corvette. Notice what is called the wide five wheels. These were fairly common at one point.

It takes a lot of tires to run 12 hours at Sebring. These tires are all for one car. More important, the car needed even more tires than you see here.

The best part of factory wheels is that they've been tested to ensure that they can take the loads without breaking. This testing doesn't always take place with aftermarket wheels.

Left: Would James Bond drive a car with billet aftermarket wheels? *Above:* The Panoz uses a brace above the engine to give the car some highly desirable stiffness. You can see how the bar over the engine bay is tied into the roll cage structure. Designing a cage for a racecar is a highly complicated task.

Above: One alternative to expensive alloy wheels is to find a stock wheel from another model of your marque. This Mercedes uses a later model wheel for vintage racing. *Right:* During the 1970s and 1980s, Porsche used an interesting system for racing. As the tires and wheels became wider, Porsche simply extended the fenders a little more. Eventually they got to the point of this Porsche 911 RSR. These huge fenders define the Porsches of that era.

Go karts actually have four springs. They just happen to be the tires on each of the four corners. The professional race teams actually measure the spring rate of the tires. They then try to match them so they can replicate a particular setup in the future.

Sway Bars: Sway bars are used to limit chassis roll and to fine-tune the balance between understeer and oversteer. Sway bars have a minimal effect while you're driving in a straight line so you can limit cornering roll with very little effect on ride comfort.

Sway bars increase the weight transfer during cornering. A stiffer bar will increase the vertical load on a tire. Most street cars don't allow for adjusting the sway bar. Often times you can swap sway bars around from model to model, or you can simply purchase an adjustable aftermarket sway bar.

Shocks: Shock absorbers are really the last thing you should change. I know that it's usually the very first thing people change, but that's because the shock companies do a lot more advertising than the spring companies. They're also a lot easier to change than springs and sway bars.

One very important thing is that shock force is dependent on the velocity of the shaft. Road bumps cause rather high velocities and cornering usually involves low shaft velocity. In other words, controlling body roll is an issue during low shaft velocity. Road irregularity is an issue with high shaft velocity.

If you do decide to change shocks, you have a variety of choices.

Single Adjustable shocks allow either rebound adjustment only or adjust rebound and compression together. This is good for most tuning. Many people don't need much more than this.

Two-Way Adjustable shocks allow adjustment of rebound and compression independently. This is a powerful tuning tool, but very confusing. Plan on a lot of testing sessions if you make this choice.

Four-Way Adjustable shocks allow adjustment of rebound and compression independently, plus low- and high-speed adjustment. This is way too serious for most people. You'll definitely need help from a professional if you want to install and tune these.

Footprint Shape

Remember that the contact area of your tire is a function of the weight of the car. It has absolutely nothing to do with the size of your tire. You can put really huge tires on your car but you won't get any more rubber coming into contact with the pavement. It's all about physics. We can, though, alter the shape of the contact patch.

Camber: Camber is nothing more than the angle of the tire in relation to the pavement. If the tire is perfectly perpendicular to the pavement we say that it has 0-degrees of camber. If the top of the tire leans in we say that the car has negative camber. If the top of the tire leans out we say the tire has positive camber. Check out the drawings below for an example of this.

Now comes the real trick. We measure the degrees of camber while the car is sitting still. Our concern though is about what happens as the car is moving.

A round contact patch is best for cornering. In order to keep the tire contact patch round, the patch needs to be aligned perpendicular to the forces of gravity and lateral acceleration, which might also be called the side force as you go around a corner.

This is the reason racing cars use so much negative camber. They need to have the outside tire perpendicular to the track as they go around a corner. In other words, they need to have the dynamic camber setting at 0-degrees as they corner. In order to get this they have to set the static camber at around -4 degrees.

In a turn, the outside tire will always carry more of the load than the inside tire. This means that during a turn, the lightly loaded inside tire will actually be cambered the wrong way. This really isn't a problem since the tire isn't being asked to do a great deal. You need to keep the *outside* tire as close to perpendicular as possible. That's the tire being asked to do all of the real work in a turn.

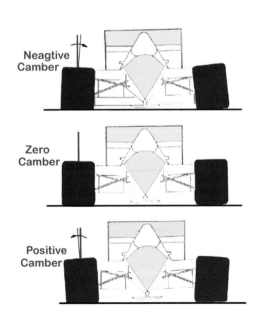

Neagtive Camber

Zero Camber

Positive Camber

When the Porsche 911 fenders got to this point, Porsche simply added running boards to the car. No one seemed to notice that running boards were last used in the 1930s.

Camber Curve: Negative camber increases cornering power. In most modern cars the suspension geometry is designed to increase negative camber as the suspension is compressed. That's exactly what we want. This change in camber is called the camber curve.

The rate of gain will depend on the application. The gain in race cars is usually formidable because there is limited suspension travel and the driver can usually cope with the resulting camber thrusts. The average street car has around .5 degree per inch of suspension travel in the front and 1.0 degree in the rear.

The rear curve is generally greater because the driver won't feel the camber thrust through the steering wheel. Also, most street cars are designed to have more rear grip. The average street car is designed to understeer.

Changing the camber curve will definitely change the handling of your car. The problem is most people don't realize when they're changing it. Most people recognize that when the car is lowered you're going to have to align the car to correct the static camber setting, or the amount of camber when the car is sitting still. The problem is that you've also changed the camber gain curve. That's why lowered cars sometimes handle worse after the modification then they did before.

This problem is especially common with a strut suspension. You need to pay particular attention to the ride height angle of the lower control arm and how much the angle changed when you lowered the car.

Slip

A great part of what we call handling is really the correlation of the car's direction to the driver's steering inputs. The problem is that not all steering inputs come from the driver. They can also come from the following three items.

Toe: When two wheels on the same axle are pointing straight ahead, that axle will go straight. When the two tires are pointing in opposite but equal angles, the axle will also go straight ahead. However, the steering behavior changes once steering input is made. We can thus preset small angles into the car to tune the handling. These presets are called toe angles.

Toe-out amplifies the steering induced output. When you start to make a turn, the outside wheels begin to load and the inside wheels unload. This means the outside wheel has more effect on the steering, since it has better grip. Also, since the inside wheel is already turned in the desired direction, the car will be quicker to respond to steering input.

Toe-in has the opposite effect. Instead of amplifying the outputs from steering, toe-in will dampen the effects. That's the reason most cars have rear toe-in. Toe-in at the rear slows the oversteer yaw-rate.

Toe-Out = More responsive but less stable
Toe-in = More stable but less responsive

Ackerman: The Ackerman effect is when the inner wheel turns more than the outer. Ackerman is really a toe-angle change that's caused by the steering geometry. The toe-out changes as the wheels are turned. This is done to improve

Above: *Even today the tire and wheel package defines the whole car. This is a Panoz that was running in the American Le Mans Series (ALMS) just a few years ago. The size of the tires is restricted so the fender flares don't have to be quite so large. Also, this car was designed around the tires, as opposed to the Porsche 911 where the basic body shell was modified to meet the tire technology of the day.* **Left:** *Another Porsche, but in this case a pure racing car. Notice how much effort is placed at getting the air out of the fender well. A decade earlier that wasn't a big deal. Then we learned about aerodynamics. Keep in mind that brake cooling is also a critical issue with these cars.*

tracking in tight turns.

With little or no Ackerman, the inside wheel tries to track out of the curve, which causes binding. The inside wheel attempts to track the curve when you have Ackerman. This allows freer turning. Basically, Ackerman helps on tight corners, but hurts high-speed tire grip.

Bump Steer: Bump steer is when the up and down suspension motion changes the camber angle. The camber setting changes as the tire goes through its travel. Most bump steer is undesirable, especially if it's in the front of the car. In the rear it may, or may not, be helpful.

THE CIRCLE OF TRACTION

Once you start to grasp the circle of traction, things begin to clear up. (Hey, it only took me about a decade to get a grip on this concept.) The circle of traction is all about the forces of nature—all of those good things you learned about

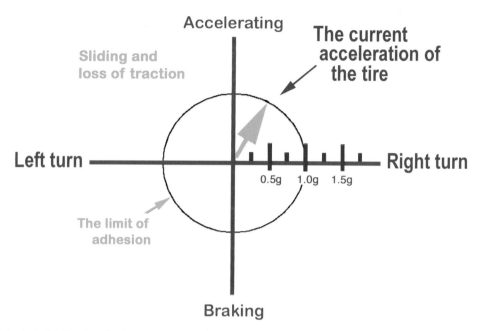

Accelerating

Sliding and
loss of traction

The current
acceleration of
the tire

Left turn — Right turn

0.5g   1.0g   1.5g

The limit of
adhesion

Braking

friction and such back in high school. If you can grasp the circle of traction concept, you can become a better driver.

Tires can generate the same force in acceleration, deceleration, or cornering. That's not true for the car, but it's definitely true of the tires. The tire really doesn't care about the direction it's asked to operate in. The coefficient of friction between your tires and the pavement is the same in all directions—well, not exactly since the footprint of the tire is never a perfect circle, but the difference is minimal.

Let's assume that a tire is capable of generating 1.4-g of acceleration force or 1.4-g of cornering force. If you're only generating 1.0-g of cornering force, then you have 0.4-g left to use for acceleration. Actually you will have a little more, because if you're working in two vectors, the sum can be slightly more than the force capacity of the tire, but for this explanation we can ignore that part of the formula. If you're going to use all of the performance potential designed into your tires, then you need to keep them operating at a very high level of *combined* forces. This means that you can combine braking, cornering, and acceleration. This isn't easy to do and should only be done on a racetrack. Even on a racetrack this won't always be necessary.

You've probably heard the term "trail braking" when people talk about driving in autocross, or on a race track. Trail braking is all about the circle of traction. It simply means that you can combine braking and turning. This is a skill that needs a lot of practice and isn't easy to develop. Before you get to that, though, you have to understand the Circle of Traction. The best way to describe all of this is to call it a circle of traction. During an autocross, for instance, you want to ride the rim of the traction circle by balancing braking, acceleration, and cornering.

As long as the combination of forces (braking, acceleration and turning) creates a force that's inside the friction circle, the tire will have traction. The friction circle is simply the area inside the circle in the illustration. When you try to go around a corner so fast that you go outside the friction circle, the tire will lose traction and you'll start to slide.

Think of the area inside the circle as the amount of traction you have available. In other words, it's a traction budget. In racing we try to spend our traction budget so as to stay as close to the limit (the circular boundary) as much as possible. In street driving, we normally stay well inside the limit so that we have lots of traction available to react to unforeseen circumstances.

Since your tires determine the amount of traction available, you want to use *all* of the capabilities of the tires as much as possible. There are many places on an autocross course where acceleration, and deceleration only use some of the tires' traction abilities. When that's the case, you can feed some lateral force into the tire. The goal is to always have your car right on the edge of traction loss—at every point on the course. The object is to be, at all times, near the edge of this circle without exceeding its limits.

If you think about this for a minute, I'm suggesting that you be just on the verge of losing control of the car while on the track, or at an autocross. Those are places where you want to use every last bit of your car's abilities—that's what being aggressive means. Just don't go outside of the circle. That's usually called a spin, although a great driver can catch the car just before the spin is about to happen.

Left: This is the right front tire on the No. 16 Dyson car. **Right:** BBS was the leader in the development of the modular wheel. The company used a forged center section with very strong spun aluminum alloy rims. In the case of this Porsche, a center-lock nut was used for endurance racing.

Coil-over units (in which a coil spring is installed over the shock absorber) have one huge advantage. By raising or lowering the lower-spring perch, you can adjust the amount of weight on each of the rear tires.

25

CHAPTER 2
TIRE OVERVIEW

READING THE TIRE'S SIDEWALL

A lot of useful information is molded into the sidewall of every tire. Included are manufacturer and tire name; section width; aspect ratio; construction; rim diameter; speed rating; load range; tread wear, temperature, and traction labeling; and a few other required designations.

If you can get through all of this you'll know more than most people who sell tires. Actually, if you're serious, you'll need to know more than the salespeople in the tire stores. A sad fact of automotive life is that most tire salespeople know very little about tires.

Size

All tires sold in the United States must meet the size standards for bead shape, width, diameter, and other parameters established by a recognized standardizing organization. World leaders among such organizations are the European Tire and Rim Technical Organization (ETRTO) and the U.S. Tire and Rim Association (T&RA). Virtually all passenger tires on the market today use the rim and tire sizing, loading, and inflating systems established by these bodies. In addition, all tires sold in the United States must also meet Department Of Transportation (DOT) standards. The letters (DOT) on the sidewall indicate this.

Several tire size designations are in use today. What you find on your tires depends on when your car was manufactured and whether it was domestically produced or was imported.

P-Metric: This is the U.S. version of a metric sizing system established in 1976. P-Metric passenger car tire sizes generally begin with P, which simply means Passenger.

Metric: This European tire sizing system is very similar to P-Metric but doesn't use the "P" designator. For all practical purposes it's the same as the P-Metric system.

Alphanumeric: This system was established in 1968 and it's based on the tire's load carrying capacity, correlated to its overall size. The tire capacity and size are indicated by letter designations from A (the smallest tire with the lowest capacity) to N (the largest tire at the time and also the highest load capacity).

An example of an alphanumeric tire size is FR70/14. The F shows both the size of the tire and the load range while the R indicates radial construction. The 70 is the aspect ratio, and 14 is the size of the wheel in inches. This is now a vintage sizing system and you will most likely find it only in reproduction tires.

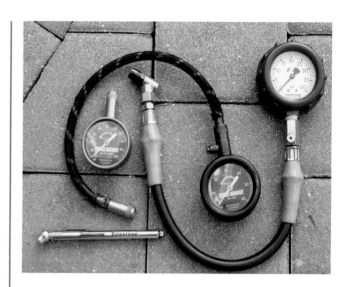

Tire gauges are available in an unbelievable variety. Some of these gauges have a bleed-down feature that allows you to bring the pressure down to the specified level by just pressing a button. You simply fill your tires and then bleed them down to the psi you want. Also, notice that one gauge only reads to 40 psi. That's just fine for my race car and the limited range makes viewing a lot easier.

Numeric: This is the oldest standardized tire sizing system for passenger car tires. It was used into the late 1960s. When this system was adopted, tire aspect ratios were either 92 or 82. There were no choices. For example, a 7.00-14 tire has a section width of 7 inches, a rim diameter of 14 inches and an aspect ratio of 92. Anything with an aspect ratio of 82 was considered to be low profile.

EVEN MORE NUMBERS?

Let's try and break all of this down even further. Eventually we'll get to something that is understandable. Remember, no one said this would be easy.

OUR EXAMPLE: 215/65HR/15

215 = Section Width

These numbers indicate the tire section width in millimeters. This is the distance from sidewall to sidewall. Keep in mind that a tire's section width varies depending on the rim to which it is fitted. The section width is larger on a wide rim and smaller on a narrow rim. Therefore, each tire is measured to specific rim width.

Don't assume that the guys at the tire store are aware of directional markings. Before I have my tires mounted and balanced, I circle all of the directional markings with yellow chalk. Then when I pick up my car I make sure the tires are going in the correct direction and on the proper side of the car. There's nothing wrong with a little paranoia when dealing with a local tire store.

ing procedure. There is a very specific procedure for determining the speed rating and tire companies must follow a standardized set of testing procedures.

R = Type of Construction

This letter indicates the type of ply construction in the tire's casing or carcass. R means radial. D means diagonal, referring to bias ply tires. B means belted for belted-bias ply tires.

15 = Rim Diameter in Inches

The "15" indicates the rim diameter in inches. It's also the diameter of the tire bead. Most tires are built to inch standards for rim diameters. Tires all over the world give the diameter of the tire in inches. Always match the tire rim diameter to the wheel rim diameter.

96H = Service Description

The service description is an alphanumeric combination consisting of two parts: a number and a letter. In this example, 96 is the load index and represents the load carrying capacity of the tire. (All passenger car tires in the United States are also marked with their actual load limit in pounds.)

The letter part is the speed symbol, H, in this example. This is the maximum speed for which the tire is rated at the load specified by the load index. A letter H rating can handle speeds up to 130 miles per hour.

DOT = Department of Transportation

DOT simply means that the tire is in compliance with all applicable safety standards established by the U.S. Department of Transportation (DOT). Each tire also features a tire identification number up to 11 numbers and letters.

This DOT Tire Identification Number (TIN), which is molded into the sidewall, designates the manufacturer and the specific plant where the tire was produced. In addition it identifies the tire line, the size, as well as the week and year the tire was manufactured. This allows your tire to be traced directly back to the manufacturing plant.

Maximum Tire Pressure/Load

All passenger tires are marked on the sidewalls to indicate maximum load capacity and maximum inflation pressure. Truck tires indicate recommended pressure for maximum loads for both dual and single application.

Don't confuse maximum tire pressure with how much air you should put in your tires. I can't believe how many people fill their tires to the maximum air pressure listed on the sidewall. The correct figures for tire pressure are gener-

65 = Aspect Ratio

This two-digit number indicates the tire's aspect ratio. It compares the inflated section height—the distance from the bead to the tread—to its section width (maximum). An aspect ratio of 65 means that the section height is 65 percent of the tire's section width.

Section Height/Section Width = Aspect Ratio

or

5.7 / 8.7 = 0.65

In an effort to make all of this easier to understand, the section width (given in millimeters) is separated from the aspect ratio by a slash.

H= Speed Rating

This indicates that the tire has been tested at 130 miles per hour (240 kilometers per hour) during a standardized test-

Someone at Kumho obviously got tired of putting air in all those race tires every weekend. They developed a system that could install nitrogen in four tires at a time. The best part is you can do it while you sit around. Who says race teams have way too much money?

Left: Kumho makes some killer slicks, but not every country gets them. This tire is only used in Europe because Kumho simply can't provide the necessary support for U.S. racing. Kumho is still a very small operation in the United States. Right: Everything is marked before the tires are returned to the teams. Even the bar code is put into the system. Notice how little weight it took to balance this tire and wheel assembly. We're talking about a tire and wheel company that pays attention to quality.

ally found on a sticker located in the door jam area. Even better, check out the specification in the owner's manual.

Harmonic Markings

Some tire companies place red or yellow dots on tires for mounting purposes. The wheels are also marked to identify the minimum radial run-out spot (low point) on the bead seat surface. Mounting the assembly in such a way

as to put these markings together is called match mounting. This method minimizes the balance weight needed to correct any remaining imbalance and the radial run-out that may occur in the wheel/tire assembly.

Most people who mount tires ignore these dots—not a good idea. If the tire company went to the trouble of finding these spots, it only makes sense for the tire shop to use them. At least that makes sense to me. Be sure to ask the

This is a lot better than those little directional markings on the sidewall of the tire. No confusion here about which tire goes where, and the direction it goes in.

Left: A tremendous amount of work goes into designing the tread. The goal is to get any water out from under the tread and then deposit it to the sides of the tire. This allows the tread to remain in contact with the pavement. That's a good thing. **Right:** Here's another Yokohama tire with just a slight variation.

Left: *This is a serious high-performance street tire. This tread pattern puts a lot more rubber on the ground during dry weather. It has some large channels to evacuate the water during a rainstorm.* **Right:** *This tire is all about extreme performance. The grooves channel the water out from under the tire. That's one reason you see huge plumes of spray coming from race cars in wet weather.*

This Kumho is only for racing in the rain. The tread design here is called a block design.

The Doran is one very serious car. It competes in the American Le Mans series in the Prototype 2 class. You don't even want to think about the tire bill.

Left: *All street tires have the size molded into the sidewall.* **Right:** *Here the all-season designation is also molded into the sidewall.*

tire store if it pays attention to the markings. That way the store will know that you're an informed customer. Maybe they'll even do the job correctly for you.

UNIFORM TIRE QUALITY GRADING SYSTEM OR UTQG

The Department of Transportation requires tire manufacturers to grade passenger car tires based on three performance factors: tread wear, traction, and temperature resistance. When you read these numbers keep in mind that the tire companies rate their own tires. No government testing is involved. The government simply developed a set of tests and has trusted tire companies to be honest in reporting their own results.

The good part is that most tire companies are honest, but variations do occur. Thus you can't compare ratings from one brand to another. You can, however, compare tire quality within a company's line of tires.

Tread wear

The tread wear number is a comparative rating based on the wear rate of the tire when tested under controlled conditions on a specified test track. A tire graded 200 might wear twice as long as one graded 100. Your actual tire mileage depends upon the conditions of use and may vary due to driving habits, service practices, differences in road characteristics, and climate.

- Greater Than 100—Better
- 100—Baseline
- Less Than 100—Poor

Keep in mind that these tread wear grades are valid only for comparisons within a manufacturer's product line. They are not valid for comparisons between manufacturers.

Let's use Bridgestone as an example. The Bridgestone Potenza S-03 has a tread wear rating of 220. The Bridgestone Turanza EL400 has a tread wear rating of 640. This means that the Turanza is going to last a lot longer than the

Above: *Drag racing slicks use a unique tire sizing system. The 33.0 means that the tire is 33 inches in total diameter. The 10.5 means that the tread measures 10.5 inches across, and the 15 means that the tire fits on a 15-inch wheel.*
Right: *You don't see too many '57 Chevys with tires this size.*

This is it. It just doesn't get much better. Put the wrong tires on this car and it would look really stupid. Just by seeing it, you just know this car is evil. It'll strike terror into the hearts of women and small children, and maybe even some men, as it leaves the line.

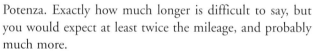

Left: *I really want to drive this to the grocery store. I really do. Notice the huge offset on these rear wheels. The wheel is designed to push the tire out from the body of the car. You can't even see the center of the wheel in this picture. When you have this much offset you better have a strong wheel.* **Above:** *Here we're back to the Big and Little combination. This is the first time I've ever seen a C4 Corvette with front tires this small. The front tires on a drag race car only have to provide steering, and very little at that. That's why you can run such small tires on the front of a dedicated drag car.*

Potenza. Exactly how much longer is difficult to say, but you would expect at least twice the mileage, and probably much more.

Traction

Traction grades represent the tire's ability to stop on wet pavement as measured under controlled conditions on specified government test surfaces of both asphalt and concrete. The traction grade is based on "straight ahead" braking tests. It does not indicate cornering ability.

A – Best: This indicates the tire performed well on both concrete and asphalt and concrete.

B – Intermediate: This tire performed well on one of the surfaces. Tire companies aren't required to state which surface though.

C – Acceptable: In this case the tire performed poorly on at least one of the surfaces.

Temperature

The temperature rating describes the tire's resistance to the generation of heat when tested under controlled conditions on a specified indoor laboratory test wheel. Sustained high temperatures can cause the materials of the tire to degenerate, thus reducing the life of the tire. Excessive temperatures can obviously lead to tire failure. Federal law requires that all tires meet the minimal requirement of Grade C.

A – Best: This indicates that the tire was able to withstand a half hour run at 115 miles per hour.

B – Intermediate: This tire was able to withstand a half hour at 100 miles per hour, but not at 115 miles per hour.

C – Acceptable: This means the tire failed to complete a half hour at 100 miles per hour.

SPEED RATINGS

Tire speed ratings must exceed the maximum speed capability of the vehicle to which they are fitted. However, not all tires sold in the United States are speed rated. Most high performance and luxury cars are equipped with speed rated tires from the factory—one of the reasons you pay extra for these cars. It's important to factor in speed ratings when replacing the tires on your vehicle. Replace your original tires with equivalent or higher speed rated tires. Do *not* downgrade speed ratings from Original Equipment ratings. That's a really stupid way to save money.

Speed ratings started in Europe where some highways don't have speed limits and extreme high-speed driving is allowed. These speed ratings were established to match the speed capability of tires with the top speed capability of the vehicles to which they are applied. Not a bad idea if you intend to drive your Porsche flat out on your holiday to the Riviera.

Speed ratings are established in kilometers per hour and subsequently converted to miles per hour. The ratings are based on

Here's one difference between a real slick and a DOT tire. If you're crazy enough to drive on the street with a slick, then you're on your own. The tire company here wants to make absolutely sure that you understand this.

A lot of the reproduction tires are made from the original molds. That means that the logo is perfect.

laboratory tests where the tire is pressed against a large diameter metal drum to reflect its appropriate load, and run at ever increasing speeds (in 6.2-mile-per-hour steps in 10-minute increments) until the tire's required speed has been met.

Speed ratings do not indicate how well a tire handles or corners. They only certify the tire's ability to withstand high speed. On the other hand you can generally assume that a tire that is V-rated is constructed of better materials, and a superior design, than a tire that is S-rated.

Over the years, tire speed rating symbols have been marked on tires in any of three ways shown in the following examples:

225/50**S**R16

225/50**S**R16 89**S**

225/50R16 89**S**

In the beginning tires had their speed-rating symbol shown within the tire size, such as 225/50SR16. Tires using this type of branding haven't been produced since 1991.

Beginning in 1991, the speed symbol is shown in the tire's service description, such as 225/50R16 89S. The most common tire speed rating symbols, maximum speeds, and typical applications include the following:

Desig-nation	mph	km/h	Usage
M	81	130	
N	87	140	Temporary Spare Tires
P	93	150	
Q	99	160	Studless & Studdable Winter Tires
R	106	170	H.D. Light Truck Tires
S	112	180	Family Sedans & Vans
T	118	190	Family Sedans & Vans
U	124	200	
H	130	210	Sport Sedans & Coupes
V	149	240	Sport Sedans, Coupes & Sports Cars

When Z-rated tires were introduced, most people thought that was the highest tire speed rating that would ever be required. Z-rated tires were capable of speeds in excess of 149 miles per hour, but exactly how far above 149 miles per hour wasn't identified. Ultimately, the tire industry had to add W and Y speed ratings to identify the tires that met the needs of new cars with even higher top-speed capabilities.

W			High Speed Sports Cars
Y			High Speed Sports Cars

While a Z rating still often appears in the tire size designation of these tires, such as 225/50ZR16 91W, the Z in the size only signifies a maximum speed capability in excess of 149 miles per hour (240 kilometers per hour) and the W in the service description indicates a maximum speed of 168 miles per hour (270 kilometers per hour). Thus, these tires actually have two speed ratings. Are you confused yet?

- 225/50ZR16   In excess of 149 mph, 240 km/h
- 205/45ZR17 88W   168 mph, 270 km/h
- 285/35ZR19 99Y   186 mph, 300 km/h

More recently the Y rating came into play. The Y-speed rating is enclosed in parentheses, such as 285/35ZR19 (99Y), and signifies that the top speed of the tire has been tested in excess of 186 miles per hour (300 kilometers per hour) indicated by the service description as shown below:

Tire sizes were a lot easier for your grandfather.

This was one of the very first low profile tires. These days it's hard to think of a 78-series tire being low profile.

- 285/35ZR19 99Y   186 mph, 300 km/h
- 285/35ZR19 (99Y)   In excess of 186 mph, 300 km/h

Most of this is meaningless for the American driver where speeds above 100 miles per hour are seldom seen, but the speed rating does indicate superior construction and materials—an important consideration when you purchase new tires. It also gives you a certain amount of bragging rights . . . if that's important to you.

Tire Repair and the Speed Rating

This one is real simple. Once you have a tire repaired, the speed ratings are meaningless. A tire repair makes the speed rating null and void. No surprise here. If a quality tire can operate at speeds in excess of 150 miles per hour, what makes you think this same tire with a patch is just as good as a new tire?

SERVICE INDICATORS

Some tires carry additional markings related to service. The Rubber Manufacturers Association (RMA) in the United States sets the guidelines.

All-Season Designation

M + S

This symbol indicates the tire meets certain requirements without the noise and rolling resistance associated with traditional deep-lug winter tires. The M+S designation also means that the tire is suitable for normal all-weather driving applications as well as for light snow. Tires that meet the requirements of the M+S designation will have better winter traction compared to those without the M+S symbol. Tires with this designation can also be used in the summer.

Severe Snow Conditions

Tires must meet performance-based criteria featuring tread pattern, construction elements, and materials which generally provide snow performance superior to that of tires bearing the RMA current M+S rating. These tires will display a mountain or snowflake symbol.

Snow tires are a highly specialized tire. They're designed for a single purpose and involve some pretty sophisticated technology. I'm going to save all of that for Chapter 5.

TIRE CONSTRUCTION

Bias Ply

The simple definition of a Bias-Ply Tire: Bias-ply tire construction uses rubber-coated layers, known as plies, composed of textile cords, usually nylon and sometimes Kevlar. The plies are layered diagonally at a 30-degree angle from one bead to the other bead. One ply is set on a bias in one direction as succeeding plies are set alternately in opposing directions as they cross each other. The ends are wrapped around the bead wires, anchoring them to the rim of the wheel. The layers of plies are then covered with more rubber to form the tread of the tire. Bias-ply tires are sometimes called cross-ply tires.

Performance and Purpose of a Bias-Ply: Bias-ply tires have very limited purpose. The bias-ply tire is an ideal tire for purposes such as tires on a towed trailer, farm equipment tires, and some purpose-built tires for extreme terrain; some forms of racing still use bias-ply tires.

Bias-ply tire casings are constructed to form one working unit. When the sidewalls deflect or bend under load, the tread squeezes in and distorts. The distortion affects the

And you thought 20-inch rims were new? It seems trends move in circles. Now we're finally back to the 20-inch rim.

tire's footprint and can decrease traction and increase wear, depending on the terrain. This tread distortion also causes abrasion from the ground surface, which reduces the life of the tire. This is why bias-ply tires are not good as passenger car tires or as tires that may see highway use.

Bias-Ply Strength: Strength of bias-ply tires is increased by increasing the number of plies and bead wires. More plies means more mass, which increases heat retention and reduces tire life.

Sidewall strength is generally less than that of a radial tire's construction and cornering is significantly less effective. This is probably one of the main reasons bias-ply tires are not used for passenger cars and trucks.

However, because of the bias-ply construction and

inherent strength of a properly inflated tire, the bias-ply is ideal for straight line towing. Any number of people still prefer a bias-ply tire for their trailers, although that number is becoming smaller all of the time.

RADIAL

The Simple Definition of a Radial Tire: The radial is constructed with rubber-coated, reinforced steel cable belts that are assembled parallel and run from side to side, bead to bead at an angle of 90 degrees to the circumferential centerline of the tire (as opposed to the 30-degree alternating application lengthwise as in bias-ply tires)—this makes the tire more flexible, which reduces rolling resistance, thus improves fuel economy. Numerous rubber-coated steel belts are then constructed into the "crown" of the tire under the tread to form a strong stable two-stage unit.

Left: While we're on the subject of trends, notice that this Model T uses modular wheels. The center section of the wheel was bolted to the rim. And how is this concept different from the latest Forgeline wheel you just bought for your Porsche 911? Right: This was actually a factory option for Buick in the mid 1950s. Below: This may be pure race car, but it's been copied on 75 percent of the street rods in the world. The best part is that it really works. You simply move the heim joints in and out to alter the caster on the car. You can also change the wheelbase with the heim joint in the foreground. And how are new cars easier to align?

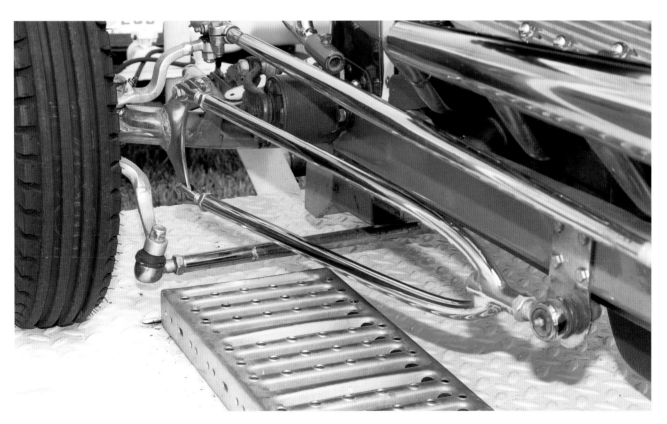

I think the S means it's a slick. Actually it's one of the smaller slicks I've seen around. Then again, the AAA midgets back in the 1950s weren't very big.

Performance and Purpose of Radial tires Radial tires are the preferred tire of choice in almost every application. The combination of steel stabilizing belts in the single-layer radial casing allows the tread and sidewall to act independently. The sidewall flexes more easily under the weight of the vehicle, providing even contact with the ground. Greater vertical deflection is achieved with radial tires. This is desirable because extreme flexing greatly increases resistance to punctures.

To increase a radial tire's strength, larger diameter steel cables are used. Larger steel cables can help reduce punctures, tears, and flats. These cables also help distribute heat, resulting in cooler tire temperatures while running and improved fuel economy. Unlike bias-ply tires, tires with larger steel cables have little negative effect on performance.

The parallel stabilizing steel belts of the radial minimize tread distortion. As the sidewalls flex under load, the belts hold the tread firmly and evenly on the ground or object, thus minimizing tread scrub and greatly increasing tread life.

When cornering, the independent action of the tread and sidewalls keeps the tread flat on the road. This allows the tire to hold to its path.

When off-road, the stabilizing steel belt design aids in greater traction by holding the tread evenly over obstacles allowing the tread of the tire to have a better chance of finding traction.

The so-common directional arrow. You can be sure that this isn't a reproduction tire. No one had even heard of the directional arrow back then. In fact, no one had even dreamed up the idea of a treadless tire.

CHAPTER 3
WHEELS

Wheels are just about the easiest thing to change on your car. You can go from stock to custom in a matter of hours. The change in appearance can be from dull steel colors to shiny chrome. Even better, you can go to some monster wheel sizes. Who cares if it destroys the handling and ride quality of the car? It looks cool. You're nothing today without a set of 30s.

Perhaps more than anything else, wheels immediately display the tastes and character of the driver. It's obvious whether the driver is a poser who just wants bling, or someone who is more serious about his or her car. From rap artist to racer, your wheels make a statement about who you are.

The wheel market is so huge it's incredible. It's also tremendously fragmented. You have everything from BBS race wheels to cheap Chinese wheels that may have been created in some rural village. Even the range of prices is wild. The cost of custom wheels range from $125 to $5,000 for a single wheel. The average is between $200 and $400 each. The tires also cost extra money—no one said this would be cheap.

There's no single trend in wheels anymore. One trend in custom wheels is to make a car or truck look like a racer. Another trend includes spinners, in which the hub of the wheel continues to spin after the vehicle has stopped. These people live in two totally different worlds, and they want totally different types of wheels.

This is curb rash and it's ugly. It's also going to cost a fair amount of money to get the wheel repaired. The good thing is that a number of companies specialize in repairing this type of problem. When the restoring is done, the wheel will look brand new.

The car companies usually provide 14- to 17-inch rims but the trend is for the large 22- and 24-inch wheels with tires to match. At the time of this writing, trends are up to 30-inch wheels . . . with no end in sight. This whole wheel thing has turned the annual Specialty Equipment Market Association (SEMA) show in Las Vegas into a wheel show. You have to really look around to find actual performance parts at SEMA.

This is some serious street bling. GM never offered Corvette wheels in chrome. I've never gotten a definitive answer about what happens to the structural integrity of the alloy under this chrome, but a lot of people feel that it weakens the structure of the wheel. You'll never see chrome wheels on a serious competition car. That may tell us all we need to know. On the other hand, chrome wheels are very easy to clean, which may account for their popularity on the street.

This is an original wheel that's been polished, and had a spinner added. The spinner may be a little too much but the owner loves it. Once you polish the wheels, maintenance is pretty easy. One of my favorites is Jeweler's Rouge. It's easy to use and not all that expensive.

This car uses 225/45ZR/17 wheels and Corvette brakes on the front. The key thing here is to make sure the wheels fit over the brake calipers. As many times as you measure, you still can't be sure until you actually try to fit things together. Don't mount your tires on the wheels until you know everything fits.

CUSTOM WHEEL MANUFACTURERS

Manufacturers of custom wheels design and create them for all makes of cars, trucks, and SUVs. There are rims manufactured for luxury cars, economy sized cars, luxury SUVs, and work trucks. Whatever you might want on your vehicle, somebody is sitting over a computer designing that wheel.

There are different manufacturing procedures for making custom wheels. There are one-, two-, and three-piece custom wheels. The combinations for design and manufacturing are endless. Any of these can be a strong and round wheel, and any can be an absolute piece of junk. It all depends on the care, and engineering, that goes into the wheel. The trick is trying to figure which company is producing a quality wheel, and which company is mainly concerned about producing the cheapest wheel possible.

Creating a one-piece custom wheel requires a mold of the desired design, a big hunk of aluminum alloy, a melting procedure to make the alloy pliable, and, finally, the casting process.

This is a Weld wheel based on the old Halibrand design. The polished aluminum wheel gives the car a nice patina. Chrome would simply be too much for this street rod.

After the wheel is cast, it goes through a finishing process, an air leak test, and then normally gets painted.

When creating two-piece wheels, a rim is created by spinning and then welded to the center. After the wheel and the rim are welded together they're inspected (we hope) and then shipped. Some of the bottom feeder wheel companies skip the inspection process and just ship the wheel out to you. They let the customer do the actual testing. Hey, why do you think that wheel was so cheap?

The process of creating a customized wheel to exact specifications and standards isn't easy. The wheel must be perfectly round with no defects in order for it to function properly. A misaligned custom wheel will ruin a vehicle and is a thing to avoid.

Keep in mind that a lot of the advertisements in magazines are simply from marketing companies who import generic cast wheels from China and re-brand the product as their own. They have little or no control over the actual manufacturing process and many don't even care about the quality. Just think about how many names you see for custom wheels these days. Isn't offshore manufacturing wonderful?

These wheel-marketing companies also know the golden rule of magazine publishing. No magazine shall ever question the product, or an advertiser, or even a potential advertiser. There's a more recent addition to that basic rule and it says that no one shall ever mention a product in a magazine unless that company buys an ad. Now you understand why no magazine will talk about the total lack of quality in aftermarket wheels. Hell, with some of these wheels you're lucky to even get a round one. We won't even talk about structural strength. It's an ugly world out there.

AFTERMARKET WHEEL SIZES

Aftermarket wheel size varies according to the car or truck that rides on the rim, not to mention the desired effects of the person making the changes to the car, motorcycle, truck, or off-road vehicle. Do you want a change in performance, or do you want to look good on cruise nights?

These are some very rare wheels. These were original equipment for the GT500 KR. This owner opted out of reproduction tires for improved ride and handling. While reproduction tires really look nice, they also ride and handle like an old tire. Does that surprise you?

Another wonderful rat rod with totally correct tires and wheels. What's even better is the grungy black bearing cap on the axle. Oh, I almost forgot about the black nasty lug nuts. This is the way rods used to be built. If you're going to do a repro, do an authentic one. This one is correct right down to the bias-ply Firestones.

Hankook has been making small slicks for a few years now. This one is mounted on a three-piece wheel for a formula car. Actually, this is also a shameless plug for Hankook since I use them on my Lola.

Some wheels, such as 15-inch wheels, are for smaller vehicles and, depending on the tire and rim combined with the car brand, can have a drastic effect on the look of the car. The effect on the handling can be just as dramatic, so be careful.

Then there are some car owners who prefer the look of a large car on smaller rims and tires. I've actually seen a full-size Chevy riding on 13-inch rims. I'm not even going to comment on the safety of that particular combination.

Seventeen- to 19-inch wheels are typical sizes these days. Sizes can be dressed up by chrome, gold, painted, or black anodized rims. A popular wheel size for many Escalades is 22 inches. These wheels are often paired up with a regular profile tire and spinning rims. The SUVs generally have more than enough room within their wheel well to accommodate a larger rim and tire combination.

We're to the point nowadays where some wheel manufacturers have developed 30-inch rims. That's big. These monster wheels are typically used on SUVs, but may be used on cars if some adjustments are made. They are also generally used with a very low profile tire. When it comes to wheel jewelry, there is no end in sight.

FORGED, BILLET, AND CAST WHEELS
Forged Wheels
Forged wheels are the gold standard in the wheel industry. Forging uses intense heat and pressure to form the alloy material into a wheel. This produces a wheel that can be up to 300 percent stronger and lighter than a cast wheel.

Forged wheels take advantage of what happens when metal is cold-worked. Cold-working doesn't necessarily mean you'd want to touch the materials while they're in process, it just means that the procedures are done at a temperature just below the metal's melting point.

When a load is applied to a metal object, it deforms slightly. When the load is removed, it regains its original shape. This happens because discontinuities move a little, and move back. If the load is high enough, the discontinuities will move until they reach the edge of their crystal structure, or until they run into another discontinuity.

Generally these discontinuities move one atom at a time, and their movement is guided by the regular structure of the crystal. If a discontinuity in the structure runs into another, the regularity is interrupted, and they may become tangled, unable to return to their starting position. This has two effects:

BFGoodrich supplies the Skip Barber School with tires. The dots that you see running across the tread of the tire are a way to measure the depth of the tread.

This is all about the 1960s. This reproduction Grand Sport Corvette uses American Racing Torq-Thrust wheels and Goodyear slicks. This isn't totally accurate, but it sure looks nice.

Another set of Avon slicks, this time on a small-bore sports racer. The real trick with these old vintage racers is to find a tire that is close to the original size. If you start altering the size, you're going to completely change the handling of the car.

The wheels are both by Forgeline, but one has a Michelin tire while the other one has a Hoosier. The most interesting, though, is how different the offsets and backspacings are. Here you can readily grasp the importance of measurements. The big advantage is that the offset can be changed rather easily on these wheels. The variations are endless with three-piece wheels.

–When the load is removed from the metal, it will not return to its original shape.

–The metal is more resistant to deformation in the future, because there are fewer discontinuities able to move around.

The idea behind forging is to get the right number of discontinuities tangled around each other, with crystals oriented in the right direction, so that the metal is strong and resistant to further deformation. This is a delicate balance, because too much cold-working makes the metal brittle, and it will fracture under load instead of absorbing loads.

You can see how this works for yourself: Bend a paper clip back and forth many times until it breaks. It begins soft, and then gets stiffer, before finally fracturing.

Forging also changes the shape and alignment of the crystal structure. When molten metal solidifies, its grain (in the sense of grains of sand) structure is non-directional, amorphous. As metal is forged, these grains are stretched in the direction of deformation, making them more like the grain of wood. The metal is formed so the grain goes in the directions where strength is needed most.

Left: This is the classic. An MG with wire wheels and Dunlop racing tires. Be still my beating heart. If you're going to race on these old wheels you better check all of the spokes on a regular basis. Steel wheels, or even better, alloy wheels, would be a better engineering choice, but people who use MGAs in vintage events are more often more interested in the cool factor of wire wheels. *Right:* Here we have the Italian version of the vintage dream. These are Dunlop tires in the 6.00L – 15 version. Obviously this owner didn't bother to paint the lettering white. Maybe that's because he spent all of his time cleaning the chrome spokes?

The forging process, because of the vast pressures involved, compacts the metal, eliminating porousness and the voids that can be a source of cracks or corrosion. The result is that less metal is required to achieve a given strength, meaning a lighter wheel in the end. Forged wheels are just better products.

Billet Wheels

Billet wheels are machined from a solid piece of material. Billet wheels are generally expensive to produce because of all the wasted material. I know one wheel company that makes as much money from selling scrap aluminum as it does from selling wheels.

A recent trend has been something called a forged billet wheel. If the alloy is simply a casting, you need to be concerned about the strength of these wheels. The cost of manufacturing a true billet wheel, where most of the alloy ends up as waste, is extremely high.

These concerns lead to the idea of forging of the basic billet. In other words a billet, or an ingot of aluminum, is forged into something that resembles a wheel. This forging is then machined to final finish. This process allows wheels to be

built with much less material (allowing for lighter weight) since the forging process makes the metal stronger.

Cast Wheels

These are the bottom feeders of the wheel industry. You just can't make a wheel much cheaper than this. Casting is an inexpensive way to produce alloy custom wheels. Basically, a cast wheel is created by pouring molten aluminum into a mold. The metal takes the mold's shape as it cools and hardens.

There are actually three types of casting methods.

Low Pressure or Gravity Casting: This is the most common form of wheel manufacturing. Liquid metal is poured into a mold and allowed to harden until the finished wheel is cool enough to be taken out of the casting.

Counter Pressure Casting: Opposite to low-pressure casting, the liquid metal is not poured; rather it is sucked into the mold using a vacuum. This reduces impurities, making the wheel much stronger than a low-pressure cast rim.

High Counter Pressure Molding: In this case, the molten alloy is forced into the mold under pressure. This eliminates voids and air bubbles. This technique produces the strongest cast wheel.

45

*Left: Yet another MGA with vintage Dunlops, but in this case they're 5.50L – 15. From a purely practical purpose these wheels are far superior to an old wire wheel. They just don't have the same visual impact. **Right:** Porsche never made this type of wheel. All of the Fuchs wheels were one-piece forged. The wider Fuchs wheels today can cost more than a used car. The solution is to cut the center out of a narrow Fuchs and then attach spun-aluminum rims. You then have a 10-inch-wide wheel at a reasonable cost.*

Each method has its place in today's market. A wheel manufacturer selects a particular method according to the weight, strength, finish, and, most important, cost. Naturally, the more sophisticated and costly methods produce lighter and stronger wheels but at a higher price.

Cheap gravity castings tend to be porous. Voids tend to form during the casting process and this is where cracks begin. Larger, chunky grains may beget larger voids, and cracks along crystal boundaries will have farther to travel.

All these points mean that cast wheels must contain more metal to achieve acceptable strength. This means that cast wheels are generally heavier than forged wheels. Still, cast wheels can be made to a high standard if close attention is given to the quality of the casting processes. The vast majority of aftermarket alloy wheels are cast, and they provide many years of decent service. Then again some of the cheap stuff is really nasty. Be careful.

WHEEL LOAD RATING

The United States Department of Transportation sets standards for wheels used by the original automobile manufacturer, and each manufacturer uses additional standards to ensure quality. No such standards, however, exist for after-

market wheels. There are some industry norms, and the better aftermarket wheel manufacturers follow them. Others don't even know what these standards are since their main job is opening cartons of wheels that arrive from some rural village in China.

In other countries, notably Germany and Japan, the governments tightly regulate the aftermarket wheel industry. Most wheel companies in the United States fear government regulation and have enlisted the support of SEMA. SEMA would like to avoid government control of the aftermarket in the United States, so they formed a group known as the Wheel Industry Council (WIC), which has undertaken the creation of a set of standards for the aftermarket wheel industry.

The WIC's goal is to educate consumers and industry members about wheel safety and quality. It is, in a sense, trying to promote an effective self-policing of the industry. Low quality products reflect poorly on an entire industry. It hopes that by publishing standards the council can avoid government regulation.

The WIC is coordinating its efforts with the Society of Automotive Engineers Aftermarket Systems Group and with regulatory agencies in other countries to develop a

Left: Drag racers use such low air pressures so the tires can easily spin on the wheels during the launch. The solution is to actually bolt the tire to the wheel. The bolt goes through the wheel and screws into the bead of the tire. Several companies make kits for this if you're a little shy about drilling your new wheels full of holes.

Below: This is a Weld Racing wheel with a Moroso tire. Moroso is a very small player in the world of drag racing tires.

This is a Weld wheel. The interesting point here is that the owner spent a lot of money on the wheels and the Mickey Thompson tires, then skipped on new wheel studs. The studs on this wheel don't even exit the lug nuts. You should have at least the diameter of the stud showing past the lug nut.

standard that will have wide acceptance and foster international marketing of quality products. A standard has been drafted by the WIC, but refining and approving it is a long process. Remember, we're asking companies to adhere to some very basic quality standards. At this point they simply recommend that people read Aftermarket Wheel Specification (SAE J2530). More information on the WIC can be found at www.sema.org. Don't look for much progress in this area.

MODULAR VS. ONE-PIECE WHEELS

Three-piece, or modular (often called composite), wheels came into vogue in the 1970s. The rim sections for three-piece wheels are normally spun from disks of aluminum. These rim sections offer the ability to custom-tailor wheels for special applications that might not be available otherwise. The rim sections are bolted to the center section to form a wheel.

When forged centers are bolted to the spun aluminum rims the result is a strong, lightweight wheel. Additional benefits included flexibility of fitment and reparability. Rims can be built for nearly any width or offset, so if you only need eight wheels for your racing program, manufac-

Left: *This is a lot of tire and wheel. Then again, this car has a whole lot of motor. This wheel has a tremendous amount of offset. The rim is designed in such a way as to provide some extra strength without adding a lot of weight.* **Right:** *The reason for the little narrow tires is that the rolling resistance is minimal. Since you don't have to steer a great deal, drag racers can use narrow tires on the non-drive wheels.*

turing them is a piece of cake, and the costs are quite reasonable. Most high-end composite wheel manufacturers deal in such small volumes that custom sizes and unique offsets are a regular part of their business.

In the beginning, these modular wheels provided several benefits. At the time, forging a one-piece wheel just wasn't economical. Porsche's factory-forged Fuchs alloy wheel, especially in the wider sizes, was considered special, but extremely expensive. That's one reason BBS was one of the early forces for three-piece wheels. At one time BBS supplied a huge number of racing Porsches with wheels.

A damaged rim could be replaced separately, making it cheaper to keep going in the rough world of racing. A three-piece wheel's advantages of exact fitment and reparability still remain today. Unfortunately, though, manufacturing a composite wheel is extremely labor intensive. A human must assemble the three pieces. Humans are slow, and ultimately cost a lot more than a machine.

A one-piece forged wheel is comparatively more expensive initially. The process, however, is faster so these extra costs can be spread out over a larger number of wheels. In a one-piece forging, all the material is structural. There are no bolts, no separate rim pieces to be bolted together, and

no extra flange material necessary for the bolts; a one-piece wheel may be a pound or two lighter than a three-piece wheel the same size and shape.

CENTERING THE WHEEL

This is critical. Pay attention. The wheel has to be centered on the axle, or hub face. Long ago, the lug nuts or the wheel bolts were used to center the wheels. This led to all sorts of problems, but these problems can be summarized by simply saying that centering was usually less than perfect, and the stress on the wheel bolts or studs could be enormous. I'm not aware of any factory passenger car wheels being made that are lug-centric.

Wheels now feature a design known as hub-centric. With a hub-centric wheel, the center hole is precisely sized where it meets the wheel hub. When the wheel is installed and the lug nuts are tightened, the raised center section of the hub fits directly into the hole of the wheel. With a hub-centric design, the lug nuts no longer support any of the vehicle's weight. The wheel is supported by the precision fit between the hub and the wheel's center bore.

The wheel bolts, or studs, then serve simply to hold the wheel onto the hub. If the studs were required to absorb vertical forces, they would be loaded in single shear. This is the weakest arrangement for any fastener. Factory wheels are all machined to fit their specific application and some of the better aftermarket wheels are as well.

Hub Rings

Many of the aftermarket wheels rely on centering rings. This means that instead of machining wheels for each application, the centering hole is machined to a generic size. Then a variety of inserts are used for different cars.

This is obviously easier (meaning cheaper) to do, and makes maintaining an inventory of a complete wheel line much simpler and less costly. If you buy wheels that use centering rings, make sure these rings fit snugly in the wheels. If they are loose enough to fall out, how accurately can they be locating your wheel?

Hub rings are usually made of hard plastic or metal and fit between the wheel and the hub. These hub rings center the wheel (more or less) on the hub ensuring that there is no run out when the wheel is installed on the vehicle.

Some tire shops automatically remove centering rings to balance a wheel. They often forget to replace them. Your hub-centric wheel will turn into a lug centric wheel because of this mistake. Keep in mind the fact that just because a wheel bolts onto a car doesn't necessarily mean it actually fits.

SOME IMPORTANT MEASUREMENTS
Backspacing

Backspacing is the measurement from the inside of the rim edge to the edge of the mounting surface. Putting a yardstick across the backside of the wheel and measuring the distance between the mounting surface hub and the horizontal straight edge can measure it. Backspace is generally

Here's an example of the correct wheel studs. This is the way it's supposed to be. The stud must exit the lug nuts. Even better are the grade-eight bolts that were used for assembling the various parts of the wheel. This person knows what they're doing.

expressed in inches.

Determining the amount of backspacing will help you determine the amount of wheel offset. This information is useful in determining what wheel will fit your car or truck, especially if you want to replace a set of wheels that fit correctly with another set of the same size but are a different style. The measurement is best done with the tire off the wheel.

Offset

Offset is the location of the flat mounting surface of a wheel relative to the wheel's centerline. Negative offset means the

Left: When you own a 1965 Mustang you might want to dress it up, but not make a radical change. Wheels are one nice way to do that. Right: The off-road folks run some serious offset. They generally run very wide tires with almost minimal backspacing.

mounting surface is toward the center of the car, positive offset means it is toward the outside of the car, or the wheel is pulled in toward the center. Offset affects many things other than just whether the wheel sticks out past the fender.

The wrong offset can cause rubbing problems when the suspension is compressed or the wheel is turned. Off-set affects the steering geometry's scrub radius, possibly leading to problems with torque steer or self-centering characteristics. In addition this offset also affects the suspension's motion ratio, which directly determines the effective spring and damper rates.

In a heavily loaded vehicle, or one with extreme changes in offsets, wheel-bearing life can be potentially affected. This is because you're putting loads on the wheel bearings that no engineer ever envisioned. It's very, very important that wheels with the proper offset be used. The alternative may be buying wheel bearings by the case.

Brake Caliper Issues

While not directly a matter of offset, brake caliper clearance is a related issue. If you have, or plan to have, big brakes on your car, be sure that the wheels you are going to use will actually fit over the brake calipers.

Spacers are available to solve this problem but it's best to get a wheel with the correct dimensions to meet your offset specs and still fit your brakes. Consulting the wheel and brake manufacturers ahead of time is wise. Many aftermarket brake companies even have templates of their brakes available that you can easily check against any wheel.

Staggered Fitment

A staggered fitment means that the wheels on the back of your car are a different size than those on the front. Wider wheels are usually run on the back. One example might be to have 19x8 wheels on the front and 19x9.5 wheels on the rear.

This is typically done on rear-wheel-drive cars, such as Infiniti G35, Nissan 350Z, BMW, Mercedes, Audi, Ford Mustang, and others. Running wider wheels on the drive wheels means more grip on acceleration, and, from an aesthetic perspective, larger wheel lips.

A staggered fitment can also mean larger diameter wheels on the rear, such as 17-inch diameter on the front and 18-inch diameter on the rear. Some examples of this would be aftermarket Acura NSX and Chevrolet Corvette wheels.

LUG NUTS AND WHEEL BOLTS

Another thing to consider when new wheels are purchased is proper lug nuts or bolts. A lot of aftermarket wheels require special lug nuts. Lug nuts can be either flat, tapered (generally at 60 degrees), or ball seats, meaning the mounting surfaces are flat, tapered, or spherical (ball shaped).

For example, most Hondas have ball lug seats from the factory, while most aftermarket wheels have a tapered lug design. If you buy aftermarket wheels for a Honda make sure you get the proper lug nuts for the wheel.

Also make sure to keep a set of lug nuts that fit your spare tire. Too often the aftermarket lug nuts necessary for your fancy wheels won't allow you to mount your spare tire. Try mounting your spare before you actually need to use it . . . you really don't want to know why I'm aware of this problem.

In addition to wheel mounting, surfaces can vary in thickness, which means that longer or shorter wheel studs or bolts may be required. I have three different sets of wheels for my Lola race car and none of the wheel bolts are interchangeable. Each set of wheels requires its own specific set of wheel bolts.

A major concern here is that there's adequate engagement between the lug nuts and studs or wheel bolts and the hub. Inadequate thread engagement could lead to the threads stretching, stripping, or loosening. Any of these things could lead to the wheel coming off.

There's agreement that it's hard to have too many threads engaged, but no one is willing to state a minimum. Robert Wood, of Wheel Enhancement, has said he likes to see at least one diameter of engagement. For example, a 12mm-diameter fastener should have 12mm of threads engaged.

The Southern California Timing Association, which governs the racing at Bonneville, requires at least ⅝ inch of thread engagement. It also prohibits the use of closed-end lug nuts, presumably to allow measurement, but also encouraging full engagement. It's likely your sanctioning body's rulebook will have something in it about wheel fasteners.

Wheel Locks

Wheel locks are stupid. Over the years I've had to break hundreds of them off because owners had no idea where the key was. Hell, most didn't even know they had wheel locks on the car. In that same period of time I've never heard of owners having their wheels stolen.

Think about having a flat tire during a rainstorm. Do you have any clue where the key to the wheel locks might be? When I buy a new car the first thing I do is throw the locking lug nuts out and replace them with the same ones that are on the rest of the wheel studs.

Black is the new chrome. Once chrome and billet wheels became common, a group of early adopters just had to move to black wheels. Wheel trends come and go. The only thing that doesn't change is the need for a strong wheel on your car. Structural integrity is more important than the look, and it's way more important than a cheap price.

CHAPTER 4
PERFORMANCE TIRES AND WHEELS

Tires are tires, right? Not really, but you're close. Race tires are just like other tires but the goals are different. Actually there are a lot fewer goals when it comes to race tires. Racing tires have only one real purpose: they need to stick to the pavement. When your tires stick to the pavement, your car goes fast. It's that simple. Sort of.

Race tires don't need to last very long—and they don't. They don't even need to work very well in the rain since there are special tires designed just for racing in the rain.

The one thing I should make clear is that when I speak of performance tires in this chapter I mean tires that are used in competition. These are not high-performance tires that are used for cruising down I-5. These are the types of tires that you're going to use to prove that your car is faster than anything else on the track, and that you're a better driver than anyone else behind the steering wheel.

ROAD RACING AND AUTOCROSS TIRES

Road racing and autocrosses have a lot in common. I know there are a lot of nuances but they have more in common with each other than they do with tires for drag racing and drifting. This race tire group can be divided into three smaller slices.

DOT Tires: These are also referred to as R-compound tires. These tires meet all of the legal requirements for a street tire and conform to all of the necessary United States Department of Transportation requirements. It just so happens that they're race tires as well.

Slicks: These tires meet no known legal requirements. They are designed to do one thing: go fast. In most cases there is a big note that's molded into the sidewall of the tire that says they are not legal for use on public roads.

Rain Tires: It's a little hard to believe but the rain tire wasn't invented until 1983. Then again, up to 1984, race car tires had tread. Once the tire companies went to slicks they had to figure out how people could race in the rain. Rain tires are designed to do only one thing: go fast on a rain-drenched racetrack.

SOME VERY BASIC IDEAS
New Tire Break-In
Breaking a new set of race tires in is critical. The first laps

Here we have the ubiquitous Weld wheel with a Mickey Thompson tire. Even though this car isn't a racer, the owner loves the racer look. I just love the fact that the inner fender well is finished to the same standard as the outside of the fender. You'll also notice that this car has front disc brakes, something not available in 1957.

I think Mickey Thompson and Weld have a hold on the drag race market. They seem to go together like Mickey and Minnie. Notice the placement of the valve stem. You have to have a really wide wheel to do this. Also, the wheel studs are the correct length.

on the tire will determine the durability and competitive life of your race tires. The first session should consist of 10 to 15 minutes of running, or about four to seven laps. The early part of the session should be run at an easy pace, with the speed gradually increased until the end of the session.

Each lap should be approximately 7 to 10 seconds faster than the previous lap. The goal is to have the tire temp as high as possible on the last lap without "shocking" the tire during the warm-up laps. In essence, no wheel spin, late braking, or sliding.

The final lap of this practice session should be run at the fastest possible speed. The intent is to achieve maximum tire temperature on the last lap. After the final lap, the car should be brought in and the tires allowed to cool at a normal rate. Ideally, the tires should be removed or the car jacked up during this cooling period. During this cooling process, the inflation pressure should be 3-5 psi higher than normal.

After you do all of this the tire should sit idle for at least 24 hours. This is possibly the most important part of the process. If you shorten this to less than 24 hours it's a waste of time. The best situation would be to allow a week before using these particular tires again.

It's important to remember that every time you drive your car, the heat you generate activates all of the various bonding agents in the rubber. As this process is repeated continually throughout the tire's life, rubber compounds gradually harden and lose flexibility, reducing the tire's grip.

Every heat cycle (every time a tire gets hot and then cools down) changes a tire to some degree, generally in the direction of making the tire harder, less flexible, and having less adhesion. Big budget racers always discard their tires based upon heat cycles, rather than just wear. That's fine because poor people like us can buy tires with lots of good tread left for very cheap prices.

These are serious tires. The car is a Formula Mazda. The whole idea behind slicks is to have as much rubber in contact with the pavement as possible.

This is a forged center-lock wheel. Center lock means that the tire is held on with a single nut. You'll also notice that a safety wire is installed to prevent the wheel from accidentally falling off should the nut loosen.

Let Other People Heat Cycle Your Tires

Now that you've discovered how much hassle it is to heat cycle your tires why not let someone else do it for you? The Tire Rack and Discount Tire will heat cycle your tires before they ship them to you.

Discount Tire (www.discounttiredirect.com) and The Tire Rack (www.thetirerack.com) use very similar systems that generate uniform heating and temperature buildup throughout the tread (something that just isn't possible on a race car because of the camber settings). They use a system of rollers that only exert a vertical scrubbing force, so no lateral force is applied. A soft temperature curve, where the tire is gradually heated and then cooled over a specified time (ambient temperature must be consistent as well), is maintained throughout the tire's depth and width.

I've seen mixed reviews on this system but everything in racing gets mixed reviews. At the very least, the theory is sound and the price is reasonable. At least it's a whole lot cheaper than buying a second set of wheels just so you can heat cycle tires and still race on the same weekend. While some people claim they didn't see any real gain, no one complained that they were slower.

Shaving Tires

Slicks work because they feature shallow tread depths (actually none) and their contact patch acts as a single unit. Any tread design breaks the contact patch into smaller elements and the greater tread depth (which is required to make wet traction possible) allows this tread to move around. This tread movement will reduce dry performance. You can't possibly optimize both dry and wet traction. The concern here is how to maximize dry traction.

Tires normally provide their best dry performance—and their worst wet performance—just before they wear out. That means a tire with no tread left is going to work really well. That's when people got the idea of actually shaving most of the tread off of their R-compound tires before they were even mounted on wheels.

The idea is that a shaved tire will provide more traction than a tire worn to the exact same tread depth after being driven for thousands of miles on the road. Think back to what we discussed about heat cycles. Here we're going to combine a tire with no tread and no heat cycles. We've just combined the best of two worlds.

Tire shaving is an effective way of permitting more of a tire's performance capability to be realized early in its life. Tire shaving removes tread rubber and reduces tire weight by several pounds. Shaving will also result in a slight increase in the width of the tire's contact patch.

The shallower tread depths reduce the tire's slip angle, increase its responsiveness, and help stabilize its cornering power by minimizing tread block squirm. Minimizing tread

Left: This is a serious piece of drag racing nostalgia—a true magnesium wheel. Very few of these wheels have survived. Magnesium may be light but it's also very fragile, and subject to serious corrosion problems. Take care of them properly and they'll last forever. Ignore them and they turn to a pile of dust. *Right:* Here's a very good example of what a flat-spotted tire looks like. The driver locked the wheel up during braking and literally wore a flat spot on the tire. This tire will never be round again. It's now just one more expensive bit of racing trash.

block squirm also reduces heat buildup and the risk of making the tire go "off" by overheating its tread compound. In many cases shaved tires actually have a longer useful life than tires that began at full tread depth.

Most DOT-legal competition tires start off with about ³/₁₆ inch of molded tread depth. All of them will benefit from shaving to ⅛-inch tread depths for driver's schools, track days, and competitive track use in dry conditions.

Tire Temperatures

If you're at all serious about racing, then you need to learn how to take tire temperatures. If you adjust your chassis just on how the car feels then you're going to make some bad decisions. It's not that you can get everything correct just by using tire temperature, but it is a critical bit of data you just can't ignore.

The key thing to keep in mind is that you're not measuring

This is one huge tire. It's a 25.5/8.5/15 Hoosier. One of the reasons that vintage cars are so fast today is because of these modern tires. Rubber compounds of this type were never envisioned in 1965.

the surface temperature of the tread, but the internal temperature of the tread. That's why you want to use a real pyrometer not an infrared thermometer. The surface temperature of the tire drops quickly. By sticking a probe an eighth of an inch into the tread you have a better chance of getting an accurate reading.

Tire temperatures are useful because they tell you what part of the tire is contacting the track. Ideally, the entire tire tread surface should be in contact with the track and working as close to equal as possible—an easy task if we traveled in straight lines, as there would be no lateral forces applied to the tire.

Use the table below as a general guideline to interpret readings and make adjustments to the car. Keep in mind that reading tire temperatures is an art. The more you do it the better you'll get at it.

Symptom	Cause
Center hotter than edges	Tire pressure too high. Reduce 1 psi for each 5° F of difference.
Edges hotter than center	Tire pressure too low. Add 1 psi for each 5° F of difference.
Inner edge hotter than outer	Too much negative camber.
Outer edge hotter than inner	Not enough negative camber or too much toe-in.
Tire below ideal temperature range	Tire pressure too high, tire too wide, or springs/sway bars too soft at that axle.
Tire above ideal temperature range	Tire pressure too low, tire too narrow, or springs/sway bars too stiff at that axle.
Front tires hotter than rear	Car is understeering (pushing). Too much front spring/sway bar, not enough rear spring/sway bar, front pressure too low, rear pressure too high, front tires too narrow, rear tires too wide.
Rear tires hotter than front	Car is over steering (loose). Too much rear spring/sway bar, not enough front spring/sway bar, rear pressure too low, front pressure too high, rear tires too narrow, front tires too wide.

Left: American Racing and the Volvo. Is there a car that doesn't look good with these wheels? *Right:* After the Corvette was beaten at Le Mans, the GM folks scheduled a meeting with Michelin. This is the result. They haven't been beaten since.

This might be an Italian car but it's got French tires. This Ferrari uses what has become the standard of the racing world: Michelin tires mounted on BBS wheels.

TIRE PRESSURES

I think I spend more time at the track messing with tire pressures than any other single thing. There are no magic numbers. You just have to keep reading your tire temperatures and making adjustments. The numbers below are from BFGoodrich and they'll get you started.

Type of Car	Axle	Starting Pressures
Front Wheel Drive	Front	35–45 psi
	Rear	30–40 psi
Front Engine/Rear Drive	Front	35–45 psi
	Rear	30–40 psi
Rear Engine/Rear Drive	Front	35–45 psi
	Rear	35–40psi

Tire Pressures and Handling

Adjustments	Effect
Raising Front Tire Pressure	Reduces Understeer
Lowering Front Tire Pressure	Reduces Oversteer
Raising Rear Tire Pressure	Reduces Understeer
Lowering Front Tire Pressure	Reduces Oversteer

Tire Pressures in the Rain

When running in the rain in both autocross and road racing you'll normally need an increase in tire pressures of 6 to 10 psi from what you might run in dry conditions. Hydroplaning occurs when a wedge of water develops between the tire and road surface. This wedge can actually lift the tire off the road and eliminate traction. Increasing the pressure results in a smaller contact patch. It also helps keep the grooves in the tread open so they can channel the water out from under the tire.

VINTAGE RACING TIRES

This is fairly easy. Read the rulebook and talk to the tire suppliers. Oh, and you might want to check the credit limit on your VISA card. There are weekends where it seems vintage racers buy more tires than the professionals do at an American Le Mans Series (ALMS) race. I'm not going to suggest which brand to purchase since that seems to change every few months. The biggest concern is whether you want to use bias-ply tires or radial tires. Keep in mind that most of our vintage cars were designed around vintage tires. If you put a set of really sticky radial tires on a car that was designed for bias tires, the handling is going to be different—plan on a lot of testing.

The other thing to keep in mind is that you can slide a bias-ply tire a lot more than you can a radial tire. That will certainly increase the fun factor. This has to do with the slip angles of the different tires. Bias-ply tires have always had a much smoother curve. The radial curve is a lot sharper, although not as bad as it was just a few years back. I've always been able to hang the car out a lot more with bias-ply tires.

ROAD RACING AND AUTOCROSS WHEELS

This is where wheels can get very expensive, as you probably need more than the usual four wheels. On the other hand, most of us with race cars seem to have three or four sets of

This Porsche has the BBS wheels, but uses Yokohama tires.

There was a time when this was the world standard for racing. Almost everyone used wire wheels and Dunlop racing tires. They still look pretty menacing.

wheels for every car we own. I'm never sure why, but it just seems to happen. It's usually a deal that you can't pass up.

Autocross Wheels

Wheel choice for autocross can be really easy. You simply walk over to the fast people in your class and find out the size and brand they're using. Then buy the same thing for your car. That's what you should do—but probably won't.

Once you start investigating the choices it's a real maze. There are a myriad of sizes, not to mention offsets, to use. The key thing to remember is that weight is your enemy. A sad fact of life is that most aftermarket wheels are heavier than the wheels that came factory on your car. Most of the time you're better off checking to see if the manufacturer offered any optional wheels and then checking the salvage yards.

Vintage Wheels

The single biggest issue here is structural integrity. Old wheels break. You just can't be careful enough. I would make sure that every wheel is x-rayed at the beginning of each season. After every event, you need to clean your wheels and look for cracks. Even the legendary Porsche Fuchs wheels are starting to develop cracks after all of these years of hard use.

THE CARE OF MAGNESIUM WHEELS

We're talking about real magnesium here. This is not an aluminum wheel that's called a "mag" wheel. This is the real deal. If you own these wheels you hate them. OK, you might like the way they look, but you know as soon as you put down the polishing rag they start to turn gray. When they're polished they look bright and beautiful. The problem is no one has enough time in his or her life to keep polishing magnesium.

Most vintage magnesium wheels were produced by sand casting. You should expect to find some imperfections in the castings. As far as telling whether you're looking at pitting or casting flaws, that's a tough call without seeing them. It's a safe bet that your wheels have a number of relatively minor casting flaws. It's also inevitable that they've got some pitting unless they've been stored in an airtight drum filled with oil.

Magnesium parts should always be stored in a dry area that's free of humidity. Bare magnesium wheels can be sprayed with WD40, which offers some protection. Some people store their magnesium wheels in thick plastic bags, and use a vacuum cleaner to draw as much of the air out of the bag as possible before tightly sealing them.

I've experimented with some ideas to keep my magnesium Minilites in decent shape. WD40 was one solution but it left the wheels sticky and made dust hard to remove. It also evaporated quickly. The only product that I really liked was Gibbs Brand, which is advertised as being a "mega penetrant." Eventually, I just gave up and had them painted in the original Minilite silver.

Racing slicks pick up an incredible amount of junk on the track. Everyone knows that slicks don't wear very well, but all of that rubber is deposited on the racing surface. As the next car drives by it picks up some of the rubber left by the previous cars. This set is marked so that the chassis guru can see how the tires are wearing.

DRAG RACING TIRES

Drag racing tires are made of a very soft rubber compound. They provide tremendous traction, but they wear out very quickly. The sidewalls of slicks are designed for straight-line performance, rather than cornering.

The power from the engine goes through the transmission and rear-end components, through the axles, and finally to the rear tires. The slicks try to rotate but can't do it because of the friction between the track surface and the rubber. The tire ends up spinning faster at the center of the wheel than at the outer edge near the track surface. This results in the tire wrinkling around a portion of the bottom of the tire.

As the slick wrinkles, the tire creates a larger contact patch with the ground. In very simple terms, the tire flattens out, creating a larger contact patch, and thus having better traction. What if that first application of power is too

Does it get any more American than this?

Just for fun, here are Goodyear's specifications and recommendations for its Eagle Dragway Specials professional drag racing tires. They're affectionately referred to as the "meats" by die-hard fans of the holeshot, which always "crinkles the meats." Compared to passenger car tires, drag tire numbers are extreme—and entertaining.

Tire Circumference:

Top Fuel	Rear: 117 in.
	Front: 69 in.
Funny Car	Rear: 117 in.
	Front: 73 in.
Pro Stock	Rear: 105 in.
	Front: 78 in.

Minimum Pressure (cold):

Top Fuel	Rear: 7.0 psi
	Front: 70 psi
Funny Car	Rear: 6.5 psi
	Front: 45 psi
Pro Stock	Rear: 5.0 psi
	Front: 45 psi

This is beautiful. This wheel and fender combination looks intimidating. Then we noticed how much weight it took to balance this tire and wheel. A lot of balance weights are a sign of a problem. (Well, it's really not a problem anymore, since all of the weight solved the problem.) Chances are that the wheel is the problem since Hoosier tires usually balance up nicely. Nonetheless, it might have been worth rotating the tire on the rim when the readout said this much weight was necessary.

much for the ground's friction to hold onto, though? Well, that's simple too: the tires spin, and you lose.

The soft compound of the tire (like all slicks) has a variety of traction-improving chemicals as well. Heating the tires activates these chemicals. The best way to do this is a burnout. To do a burnout, back the car up into a designated area called the burnout box that has been sprayed with water. Tap the gas to spin the tires over in the water, and then pull out just onto the dry asphalt. Holding the brake, crank the engine up to 5,000 rpm in first gear. This spins the tires hard, and as the water starts to dry off, the slicks start to heat up.

Heating the slicks releases the chemicals, and the tires become sticky to the touch. As I mentioned before, not heating the tires leads to traction deficiency, but over-heating the tires can do the same. If too many of the chemicals are released and the tires get too hot, the tire can actually become slippery. Burnouts are really an art form.

While the above may be great for a dedicated drag racer, my advice for the average person is a little different. Most of us should simply go around the water box. Do a short burnout to get the dirt off of your tires and heat them up a bit.

If you get near the water it'll get in your tread and then be thrown into your wheel well. This water will drip on your tires, and the track, the whole run. This is very dan-

gerous for the people running slicks behind you, and could get you removed from the track. Also, if you do your burnout in the water, it sprays all over everyone and everything within 50 yards of the starting line. The driver in line behind you will be a little annoyed.

Street tires may require a fairly hard burnout on the first and second pass to break them in. The rules for street car drag racing usually require a DOT tire. The street tires used in drag racing look almost like slicks with a couple of grooves cut in them, but they have a number of differences.

One of those differences is weight. Drag slicks are constructed as light as possible. A DOT, or R-compound tire is required to have a load range, and it must have that load range cast into the side of the tire. Heavier construction means more weight. An example is the Mickey Thompson 33/18.5/15LT that has an overall tire weight of 43 pounds. A similarly sized conventional M/T E.T. drag slick weighs 37 pounds.

Tires designed especially for street car drag racing aren't just a slick with a couple of grooves cut in them; they're true race tires that are designed just for their task—race tires designed from the ground up for the application. Due to the reduced tread depth and the compounds used in these tires, they should be used on dry pavement only and aren't suitable for highway use. Remember, these are specialized race tires.

Left: These are incredible wheels but people who race them a lot are finally finding cracks in the wheels. Make sure you check your race wheels for cracks on a regular basis. Vintage racing requires old wheels and really sticky tires. This combination can cause problems. *Right:* An interesting problem here is that the owner is using aluminum lug nuts. Most sanctioning bodies won't allow this. The combination works fine for the street, but at the track it can cause problems.

Left: General Motors makes some very strong wheels. They're stronger than most of the aftermarket wheels you can purchase. Plus, the GM wheels undergo some very rigorous testing. *Right:* These wheels are from Complete Custom Wheels. Over the past decade it has dominated the autocross market. The company produces a very strong wheel sold at a reasonable price.

Street slicks are typically designed as tube-type tires. There are a number of reasons for this, primarily safety. In addition, a tube helps maintain air pressure. It's not uncommon for a tubeless street car tire to deflate quickly—that even includes several of the more "streetable" types with a full complement of tread.

Tubes also enhance the reaction time, increase the stiffness of the tire, and reduce sidewall shock and deflection when launching the car. Finally, a tube helps with consistency because the tube actually absorbs some of the heat from the tire.

In street drag racing, a natural rubber tube is the best. It's not a good idea to use tubes designed for large trucks because they are not sized correctly. For the most part, each manufacturer of drag race street tires will have an appropriate tube size for a given tire.

Left: Another set of Fuchs wheels with the RSR finish. Notice here that this owner has the correct steel lug nuts. *Right:* These are big. The Goodyear slicks are 25.5/14.0/16. Notice the huge offset that was necessary. Oh, also notice the huge fender that was required to cover the tire.

Left: This is a 5.257/10.5/15 Dunlop vintage racing tire. The important thing here is that the owner used the correct size wheel studs. If anything, they're a little longer than is necessary but that's not a problem. *Right:* You just can't find this wheel at the local swap meet. This is a real magnesium drag wheel from decades ago. The interesting thing is that the tire is from Wal-Mart. The tires are Marshal, a European company that has some sort of relationship with Wal-Mart. The interesting point here is that the tire is a steel-belted radial. Not quite authentic, but still a good choice.

Mickey Thompson has six categories as recommended starting points for tire pressure. According to M/T, the actual optimum air pressure may vary significantly, depending, of course, on the variables below. The recommended baseline pressures are as follows:

ET Drag® and ET Street™

Vehicle Weight	Tire Size	Air Pressure
Under 2,500 pounds	Under 30' diameter	6 P.S.I. and up
Under 2,500 pounds	Over 30' diameter	4 P.S.I. and up
2,500 to 3,000 pounds	Under 30' diameter	8 P.S.I. and up
2,500 to 3,000 pounds	Over 30' diameter	6 P.S.I. and up
Over 3,000 pounds	Under 30' diameter	16 P.S.I. and up
Over 3,000 pounds	Over 30' diameter	10 P.S.I. and up

ET Drag Radial

Vehicle Weight	Tire Size	Air Pressure
Under 2,500 pounds	Under 30' diameter	16 P.S.I. and up
Under 2,500 pounds	Over 30' diameter	12 P.S.I. and up
2,500 to 3,000 pounds	Under 30' diameter	16 P.S.I. and up
2,500 TO 3,000 pounds	Over 30' diameter	12 P.S.I. and up
Over 3,000 pounds	Under 30' diameter	16 P.S.I. and up
Over 3,000 pounds	Over 30' diameter	12 P.S.I. and up

If you're approaching middle age this picture is going to look a little strange. The big tire is on the front. Oh, that's right, it's a front-wheel-drive drag car. This car is sitting in the staging lane. Notice how little air is in the tire. The tire is a drag racing radial. This tire could be under 10 psi in an effort to get as much rubber on the pavement as possible.

This is where the term wrinkle wall came from. The tire is a 31.0/13.0/15 slick. There is so little air in the tire that bolts are used to keep the tire and wheel together.

Left: This is more than just a legal notice, it's a reminder to use common sense. **Right:** DO6 is the designation for the rubber compound being used. The overall diameter of the tire is 29.0 inches, while the section width is roughly 10.5—not the width of the tread. The tread area on this particular tire is 11 inches. One nice thing is that all of this information is now available on the Internet. Use it.

Tire Pressures

How much air pressure is required for these tires? According to Mickey Thompson Tires, proper air pressure is critical in its E.T. Street drag tire. M/T notes that recommending air pressure isn't easy because there are so many variables involved. For example, the weight distribution of the car, transmission type, chassis setup, wheel size, and other factors add up, and they can affect operating pressures.

In drag racing, most racers feel that less is better when it comes to air pressure. While there are exceptions to every rule, higher pressures generally work best with Mickey Thompson tires. Not only do the higher pressures lead to quicker times, but they also contribute to a safer, more stable ride at the finish line.

Adjust the tire air pressure up or down in 1/2 psi increments to achieve the desired results. Use as much tire air pressure as possible for the track condition without causing the tire to slip.

As a general rule you should lower the pressure to increase traction, and increase the pressure to improve reaction time, stability, and rolling resistance. I do not recommend using tire air pressure of less than 5 psi, as stability will be severely compromised.

The wrinkle wall slick acts like a big rubber band on the starting line. The wheel starts to turn but the tire stays glued to the pavement. It's winding up like a giant spring. Eventually when the tire can no longer keep its grip on the pavement all hell breaks loose.

Balancing Drag Slicks

Static or bubble balancing may be the best approach with drag racing tires. Dynamic, or spin, balancing works only if the tire doesn't change shape. In drag racing the tire goes through a lot of changes in shape. At launch, the tire wrinkles and squats. As the car goes toward the top end, the tire begins turning into more of an oval. A static balance ensures the tire is balanced around the circumference as it deforms. Spin balancing may simply not be necessary, or even provide any benefit.

DRAG RACING WHEELS
What about bead screws or a bead lock wheel?
Either type is acceptable. The first step though is to see if you really need something. You'll need to mark the tire and wheel with a chalk (or paint) line to check for slippage. At the end of your run look to see if the wheel and tire marks are still in alignment. If they're not it means the tire has slipped on the wheel. You now have a new job for the coming week.

Wheel Rim Screw Procedure
Recommended rim screw:
3⁄16 inch hex washer head sheet metal screw - No. 14x3/4 Grade 8 or better
(Moroso or Mr. Gasket rim screw kits are acceptable)

Hole placement procedure:
Dismount the tire from the rim.

Measure and mark the placement of the screw holes spaced equal distances around the rim (up to 32 screws per side).

When you mark the screw holes make sure the holes on the outside face of the rim are directly across from the holes on the inside half of the rim.

Center punch these marks and drill pilot holes using a 13/64-inch drill bit.

Using one screw as a thread-tapping device, thread each screw pilot hole.

Examine the rim and debur the holes as necessary.

Here we have the rear tire on a front-wheel-drive car. It's going to take the older drag racers a while to get used to having the little tires on the back.

*Left: You could actually put a larger tire on this Camaro. This owner decided to go with 31.0/10.5/15 rather than the 31/13.0/15. Selecting the correct tire size and rubber compound is an art. **Right:** This is what a street-legal drag tire looks like. That's the tread that allows it to be approved by the United States Department of Transportation.*

DRIFTING

A single afternoon of drifting can destroy a brand-new set of tires. While that's a lot of fun, it's also expensive. When you go shopping for tires, look for special drifting tires. Look for a tire that has the perfect blend of traction and spin. Put hard-compound tires on your rear wheels if you want performance, and use softer tires if you're interested in showing off a huge cloud of smoke. As for wheels, most drifters like 15-inch rims on the rear because 15-inch tires are cheap.

As your drifting technique gets better, you'll probably want to upgrade your rear tires to a set with a higher grip compound. Although cheap, hard tires are fun purely for their slipperiness and ease of drifting, but they quickly become a hazard for high-speed drifts.

A common misconception is that drifters want slippery, low-traction tires. The opposite is true. Grip with reliable control even at severe slip angles is the most important attribute. A lot of the ultra-performance tires have high grip, control capability can fall off drastically beyond maximum cornering ability. A good drift tire has a flatter cornering force curve and gives the control and feedback needed for precise navigation at huge yaw angles.

Drifting, which is really the art of controlling a car while it's going sideways, requires high performance tires designed for lateral as well as longitudinal forces. Drifting is the worst-case scenario for a tire. You're putting a tire through—and past—the extreme boundaries of the traction circle: max acceleration, cornering, and braking. The key is being able to run at these extremes and maintain control during all points of acceleration, cornering, drift, and recovery.

Gary McKinney, of McKinney Motorsports, says, "Drift tires require side grip. When the tires are spinning, there's a thin line between slipping and traction. We require tremendous amounts of traction to keep the car off the wall, keep from swapping paint with the other car on the track, and win judging points for precision driving with style and flare."

CHAPTER 5
STREET TIRES

MMost tires are designed for the street. This is the huge market, and everyone wants a piece of the action. Thus, the street tire spectrum is huge. A street tire can be everything from the $19.95 tire you purchase at Wal-Mart to a highly specialized snow tire that might run several hundred dollars, and may only be available from a specialty store.

Several decades ago there were snow tires and regular tires. That was it. Over the past few decades, tire companies have continued to segment the tire market into smaller and smaller slices. Now it seems that we have tires for each day of the week.

Actually we do. My Kumho V710 DOT-approved tires are only used at the track on Sunday. I have weekday tires and weekend tires now! I don't want to think about this too much or my head will hurt.

Buying a set of new tires is like working through a decision tree. You have to make a series of decisions in order to narrow the field. The list below provides a starting point. I've borrowed this listing from The Tire Rack (www.thetirerack.com). The list not only shows how segmented the tire world really is but it gives you a starting point for your purchase.

Summer
Extreme Performance Summer
Maximum Performance Summer
Ultra High Performance Summer
High Performance Summer
Grand Touring Summer
Track and Competition DOT approved

All Season
Ultra High Performance All-Season
High Performance All-Season
Performance All-Season

This is the classic rubber band on steel look. The ride and handling with this combination is really horrible, but that's not the point. This combination has incredible street presence. Couple these rims with a Hemi and you can't be much cooler.

Left: Here's a 205/40R/17 tire on a nicely designed wheel. A 40-series profile really isn't that low, but when you couple it with a 205 mm section it is. Remember that the 40 stands for 40 percent of the section width, which in this case is only 205 mm. This means the sidewall is 82 mm high. **Right:** *Here's one more variation on the Torq thrust design. White lettering is making an incredible comeback on 1970s cars. Do I sense a disco influence? The tire here is a P225/60R/15. It's also described as an all-season tire.*

Grand Touring All-Season
Standard Touring All-Season
Passenger All-Season

Winter Tires
Performance Winter
Studless Ice and Snow
Studdable Snow

The biggest problem is that all of this fine slicing of the tire market can leave you totally confused. After all, what's the difference between an Extreme Performance tire and one called Maximum Performance? Not much.

Let's make this simple and talk in broad categories. We really have three types of passenger car tires.

Summer, All Season, Winter.

SUMMER TIRES

This is a tire for people who install snow tires when the first flakes hit, or at least live in a place that never sees snow or ice. These tires emphasize handling and high-speed driving. They're generally good in the rain, and wear decently.

Summer tires are designed for warmer temperatures and high stress use. Because of this, they have very large, stable tread blocks that are generally not very good in winter weather. In addition, the rubber compound does not maintain elasticity in cold weather. This means the grip level of the tire degrades drastically in cold temperatures, even on dry pavement. In the cold, a summer tire becomes unpredictable and feels slippery when cornering no matter what the precipitation level might be. This problem is compounded in wet or snowy conditions.

ALL-SEASON PASSENGER CAR TIRES

The best way to describe these tires is that they all have an M+S (Mud + Snow) symbol on the tire. This is also the great compromise tire. The idea is to provide you with a tire that can handle light snow and rain. This is generally done by using a more aggressive tread design than a summer tire. The rubber compounds are also more flexible in cold weather. In order to get these things, hot summer and high-speed performance are sacrificed. The same thing happens at the other end where these tires really don't handle snow.

Compared to a true winter tire, an all-season tire has shoulder blocks and groove designs that were compromised in order to meet the wear and cornering requirements of all-season traction. The tire is less aggressive in terms of winter traction and is designed to deliver a more comfort-

Left: Even the wheel lock on this Rolls Royce is discreet. The tire, however, is pretty normal. It's a Michelin P225/75R/15. Remembering that ride quality is of the essence with Rolls Royce, a 75-series tire should be no big surprise. *Right:* This tire is a Coker Classic on a beautiful wire wheel. You give up something in performance to get the correct look with the reproduction tires. A lot of classic car owners feel the trade off is worth it, while some prefer the superior ride and handling of a modern tire.

Left: This is no reproduction. This is the real deal. The cracks alone attest to that. I wouldn't want to drive on this tire, but when it comes to show-car judging it is always better to go with an original look. Clubs have to consider safety in their rules. Should this car, with an unsafe but original tire, get more points than a car that uses a safe reproduction tire? *Right:* When it comes to the Uniform Tire Quality Grade (UTQG) Standards, you have to keep in mind that the tire companies do their own testing and classification. The government simply sets the procedures for the testing.

able ride. As a result of all this, an all-season tire does not pack nor expel snow as effectively as a winter tire does.

Many manufacturers install all-season and all-season performance tires on their vehicles as original equipment, so you may not need to make a winter tire change if you live in a temperate climate. So how do you tell if you've already got all-season tires on your vehicle? Simple, just look at the sidewall for the letters M+S.

All-season tires are currently the most popular tire types for general use. These tires are designed for year-round use on dry or wet surfaces and also do well in light snow (2 inches or less). If you live in an area where winter driving

The tire here is a 245/60R/15. The fascination with wire wheels will never go away.

This is one wheel I wouldn't mind cleaning on the weekend. Chrome wheels are really easy to keep clean. Just don't let this wheel get into winter slush and road salt.

conditions consist of rain, light frost, some sleet, and the occasional light snowstorm, all-season tires may be all you need.

Anyone who is considering all-season tires for year-round or winter use needs to carefully examine his or her driving habits. If giving up winter performance to gain more tread life and avoid the hassle of changing over to winter tires is acceptable, then it may well be worth it to utilize all-season tires.

The biggest asset to all-season tires, though, is that they can perform effectively for the whole year, catering to both dry and wet driving on the road as compared to winter snow tires that are designed only to perform effectively during winter. They may help you avoid that dreaded change to winter tires that people in North Dakota face every fall.

WINTER TIRES

If you live in Canada, Minnesota, or some such other frozen landscape, you need to get serious about your winter tires. They used to be called snow tires, but sometime in the last decade snow tires took on the name winter tires. They're really the same thing. As tires become more high-tech and specialized, the snow tire is making a huge comeback.

Carmakers also are designing vehicles with more power and greater potential for speed and handling. These fast cars are rolling out of the factory on performance tires with sticky treads that are ideal in warm weather but can be an absolute nightmare in winter. Drivers in colder regions begin dreading the prospect of driving through snow and ice. I know any number of people who simply park their

If you have a wheel like this make sure you give very specific directions to the guys who balance your wheel. The weights here are nicely hidden.

BMWs and Mercedes in the winter.

An all-season tire and a winter tire are separated by temperature. When the weather gets really cold, the average all-season tire stiffens up and starts to lose grip. The rubber compounds used in a true snow tire remain pliable when the temperature drops below freezing.

The other advantage of a true snow tire is that the tread is designed to throw out the snow from between the tread blocks. As you drive down the road the snow is ejected from the tread allowing the tire to get more of a grip.

Basically, a winter tire uses dedicated rubber compounds and special tread designs. The downside is that your snow tires won't last as long as regular M+S tires. On the other hand, you'll generally only have them on your car for three to four months. Most people get several winters out of their snow tires.

Though you might be tempted to buy just two winter tires for your drive axle, this isn't a great idea. That's because mixing winter and all-season tires can lead to really poor handling balance. Two winter tires can be dangerous in skid situations since the front tires will have totally different traction than the rear tires.

Several years ago I was determined to drive my Mercedes during the winter and put four winter tires on the car. I couldn't believe the difference. I was actually able to drive a Mercedes in snow.

Smaller tires for winter?

Plus-sizing, which means choosing a larger wheel size and tire than originally specified for your vehicle, is popular for summer tires. For example, if your car specifies a wheel size of 16 inches, increasing wheel size by one inch would result in a 17-inch wheel, or plus one for your vehicle. The tire you buy will then need to have a shorter sidewall and wider tread to accommodate the same load and tire diameter.

Although many drivers are doing this for cosmetic reasons—a larger wheel and narrower tire has a sportier look—

The wheel design that just won't go away. This is an 18-inch black version. The tire is a 235/50ZR/18.

Above: *One of the real issues with wheels is the clearance you need for the brake calipers. This is about as close as you can get. Also, keep in mind that if you have any wheel flex, you may hit the caliper with the wheel. Every now and again look for scratches on your brake caliper. If you should see scratches on the brake caliper it means that your wheel is flexing while you drive. It also means you need to buy a higher-quality wheel.* **Below:** *Here is the lower end of the wheel market. The fake bolt heads are the first indication. The tire is a Nitto 245/35ZR/20. Nitto has an incredible market share in this type of wheel and tire combination. Nitto is also a pretty decent tire at a modest price.*

A FEW BASIC SNOW-TIRE GUIDELINES

Narrower Tires Are Better: Although wider tires with larger wheels are a popular look these days, narrower tires are best for cutting a path through snow and slush. It's best to go with the base tire size specified for your vehicle.

You can usually pick up a set of steel wheels at a salvage yard, eBay, or Craig's List for a reasonable amount of money. Since they're the basic wheels for your particular car, they're probably the narrowest wheels available for your car. Look up the basic information for your car and find out what is the smallest tire that was standard equipment on your car. Then get four of them to use as winter wheels.

Studded vs. Studless Tires: Studded tires generally do better on ice than non-studded tires. Studs make little difference in snow. If you regularly deal with icy roads, studded tires are the way to go. Be sure to check the legal regulations in your area, as studded tires are illegal in some states.

Remember, studded tires are noisy. Do you really need that noise if you only need studs a couple of times a year? On the other hand, if you have to endure a half dozen ice storms a year it may be well worth it. Just keep in mind that studs are very little help in snow.

Get Four Tires: Although it may be tempting to just buy two snow tires for your car, that's a bad idea. Tires react differently, and non-matching tires can deliver unpredictable handling.

In Europe, four snow tires are standard operating procedure. In the United States, we try to make do with only putting snow tires on the drive wheels.

Winter Tires Wear Faster: Snow tires use softer rubber compounds and deeper treads than all-season tires. This means that they wear much more quickly than all-season tires.

plus-sizing is a bad idea for winter tires. That's because wider tires must carve a wider path through snow; that means more resistance and drag. Instead, experts recommend using a narrow winter tire.

Narrower tires can more easily cut a path through snow and slush. You can also "minus size" your original tire size

by selecting a narrower tread and smaller wheel size. This can also save you some money, since narrower tires and smaller wheels are usually cheaper than wider tires with larger wheels.

Winter tires are generally Q or H rated. H-rated tires are rated up to 130 miles per hour. Q-tires are rated up to 99 miles per hour. When it comes to winter tires, however, the speed rating translates a bit differently. Consumer Reports says that more expensive H-rated tires generally get better performance at lower speeds in ice and snow. Q-rated winter tires are usually less expensive. It's your choice.

Is Your Tire a Stud?

Studded snow tires can get you through just about any ice storm. They can also create a lot of noise and they wear out highways. At least 10 states have banned studded tires, and a lot of others have put very strict restrictions on them. Studded tires are not popular in most of the United States.

Most tire experts acknowledge that while studs are a big help on ice, they don't make much of a difference on snow. Most studded tires require that the tire dealer imbed small metal spikes in the tire tread. While Consumer Reports says studded tires are still best if you live in a region where icy conditions are prevalent, non-studded tires are the best choice for most people. Some non-studded tires even come very close to matching studded tires for performance on ice. The latest improvements in materials and tread design have done a lot to help boost traction on ice.

AIR PRESSURE MONITORS AND OTHER FUN THINGS

Tire-pressure monitoring systems became a federal requirement for 2007. These systems are now installed on all new light vehicles, which includes passenger cars and light trucks such as sport utility vehicles and pickups.

The rules on mandatory tire pressure monitors for all cars were brought about by the TREAD (Transportation Recall Enhancement, Accountability and Documentation) Act, The TREAD Act triggered substantial growth in run-flat tire installation at the factory.

The TREAD Act was a congressional response to the significant number of fatalities resulting from the Ford/Firestone catastrophe in 2000. The Act became law in fall 2000. The legislation delegated new rulemaking authority to the National Highway Traffic Safety Administration (NHTSA) and mandated that the agency carry out a list of critical tasks.

Monitoring systems can mean more time and higher costs at the repair shop. Tires with monitoring systems require special tools and technical knowledge. For example, when wheel positions are changed on the vehicle, individual sensors must be reprogrammed. If not, the on-board computer will assign pressure data to an incorrect wheel. For customers, it means more waiting while their tires are rotated, changed, and checked, along with having to pay for the technology and extra labor required.

Monitoring-system wheels also require more care during

*Left: Another Nitto tire, but this time with an aftermarket Shelby wheel. **Right:** This is what I call Extreme Street. The wheel is cast and the tire is a 215/35ZR/18 Toyo. I'm not sure why the owner went to so much negative camber, but I suspect it was a way of fitting this tire and wheel combination under the fender. I'm not sure this would be the most pleasant car to drive but that would be missing the point with this car.*

Left: Tear-drop spotlights and spinner hubcaps. It doesn't get any more retro. The best part of this combination is that it is very inexpensive compared to some of the combinations you see around town. *Right:* I have a soft spot for naked suspension. There are a lot of times when an all-black look is more effective than the billet look. We know it's a lot cheaper. Money alone won't make a car look good.

tire mounting and demounting to avoid damaging the sensors. (Breaking a sensor can set a dealership back as much as $150.)

RUN-FLAT TIRES

I'm not a big fan of run-flat tires. They were first developed to solve some engineering problems and to reduce costs. Tire performance was almost a secondary consideration. It's ironic that one of the first cars to use run-flats was the 1997 Corvette. Actually, the run-flat was tested as an option in 1994, but few people ordered it.

Then engineers on the Corvette team were dedicated to low weight and high quality. The spare tire, and the nessessary jack, has always created rattles. When your new Corvette has a rattle you get irritated. Someone, probably over lunch, hit on the idea that by eliminating the spare you could get rid of the problem with a rattling jack.

Then, when the accounting people heard about this, they emphasized that four tires would always be cheaper than five. The fuel mileage people chimed in that by reducing weight the gas mileage would go up. The next thing you knew, the spare tire was a part of history.

Those first Goodyear run-flats were horrible tires. The car simply wouldn't handle with run-flats. Over the inter-

vening decades they've gotten much better. Now roughly 87 percent of new car buyers want run-flat tires. That's sad.

Eventually, all cars will come standard with run-flat-type tires. Such a development meshes perfectly with manufacturers' intentions to eliminate the spare wheel and all related paraphernalia from their vehicles.

SO WHAT ABOUT THE TIRES THAT CAME ON MY CAR?

The people who designed your car fully realized that it makes no sense to spend millions of dollars developing the ride and handling qualities of a new vehicle's suspension and then throw some generic tires on the car. This has resulted in either completely new tire designs or fine-tuned versions of existing designs being engineered for every new car and light truck from the beginning of the vehicle's development process.

The manufacturers are very concerned about what tires are used because tire comfort and tire performance directly correlate with the driver's overall vehicle satisfaction. Original equipment tires play a huge role in achieving the vehicle's desired comfort and performance capabilities, and greatly influence the vehicle's personality. And as vehicles

Here's another very clean, inexpensive, and very nice looking combination. The tire is a 225/55R/16 Falken all-season tire.

have evolved, so have tires. For the most part, today's cars are lighter, more fuel-efficient, and more responsive than those built a decade ago. This has caused corresponding reductions in tire weight and rolling resistance, while enhancing the tire's handling capabilities.

Unfortunately even the best tires are still a compromise. This is because the current materials and manufacturing technologies that provide many desirable tire attributes are directly opposed to other desirable attributes. For example, a hard tread compound that provides long wear and low rolling resistance also reduces traction. An aggressive tread design that resists hydroplaning or provides enhanced snow traction also generates more noise. A stiff sidewall that provides responsive handling and high-speed stability also reduces ride comfort. These opposing goals require blending and balancing the tire's comfort and performance traits until they are optimized for the intended vehicle application.

Every manufacturer prioritizes the areas that they feel are of greatest benefit to help their vehicles satisfy drivers. You

This is the old Pro Street look. The owner of this Studebaker opted for a very narrow Kumho on the front and big slicks on the rear.

can actually graph a tire's characteristics on a spider chart. These charts provide a visual means of presenting multiple performance characteristics to allow direct comparison of an existing tire's capabilities (usually established at the 100 level as a baseline) to the targets and/or realized performance levels for a new tire.

While the tire manufacturer's ultimate goal is to develop technology that allows it to expand the new tire's entire comfort and performance envelope in all directions, the tire maker is only able to expand the tire's capabilities in several areas without causing harm in other areas.

Quite simply, there are different goals for a tire that's going to be used on a luxury coupe compared to a tire intended for a sports car. Which is the better tire? In reality, neither of them is better; they're just different. Most important, both would be tuned to meet the desired personality of the car. However, if misapplied, the driver would experience a loss of performance if the luxury coupe tires were installed on the sports car, or a loss of comfort if the sports car tires were installed on the luxury coupe.

In my own case, I'm a huge fan of the Kuhmo 710 on my track car. I wouldn't think about putting these tires on my wife's BMW. Likewise, using Continentals on the Corvette would be a huge mistake. Both tires are really great for what they're intended. Putting them on a different car (one with a different purpose) would be a disaster.

Only the vehicle manufacturer and tire manufacturer working together to develop the original equipment tire can determine exactly which tire design and internal construction will produce the most satisfactory results. A tire manufacturer that builds all-purpose replacement tires will never receive the benefit of the vehicle manufacturer's insight and intent, and is relegated to producing average tires.

ROAD HAZARD PROTECTION?

Whether or not to have road hazard protection is always a good question. It's also a good way for dealers and companies to make money. I've always called the road hazard programs a type of legalized betting. When you purchase a road hazard protection contract you're essentially betting that you're going to destroy some tires.

The company offering you the contract, on the other hand, is betting that nothing bad is going to happen to your tires and at the end of the day they get to pocket the money you've paid. It's sort of ironic that with a road hazard warranty the tire company is betting that you won't have a problem and you the buyer are assuming that bad things are going to happen to those new tires you so carefully picked out.

There are times, however, when it seems that the roads are designed to kill new tires. There are potholes and trash on the roads that we drive. Tires can withstand wear and tear, but especially bad roads or conditions can leave your tires in need of repairs or even replacement. Your tire manufacturer's warranty only covers problems that are caused by what it determines to be defects.

The companies usually define this defect as a manufacturing problem, or manufacturing imperfection, which causes your new tire to fail. Companies will usually only fix a defect if they find that they caused the problem. So when you cut your tire with a nail from that construction zone you travel through every day, the manufacturer's warranty is not going to cover that. A road hazard warranty would cover that.

The road hazard warranty covers your tires when these unexpected events occur. Running over trash and hitting potholes is an everyday occurrence. Add to that the construction zones that are always popping up all over town. There are a lot of sharp objects that our tires can run over every day and most of us are fortunate to not have anything happen to our tires.

If something does happen to your tire, such as a cut or a piercing, wouldn't it feel nice to know that it is covered? Your road hazard warranty should pay for your cut or piercing to be fixed. Depending on the warranty you purchase, you can even be covered if the whole tire is destroyed. You

Left: *I'm normally not too excited about different brands of tires on the front and the rear. In this case, though, the front/rear combination is so extreme that different brands are the least of this owner's problem. The front tire of this car is on page 75 at the bottom.* **Right:** *Sometimes, a return to stock is the best solution. This owner carefully restored the stock wheel to a level of perfection GM never bothered with and the results are stunning.*

Left: *The tire here is a P235/60R/15 all-season tire. Notice the way the brake drum has been detailed just as nicely as the wheel. A lot of attention to detail is what makes this car so nice.* **Right:** *The only way to make this tire and wheel fit was to throw a lot of negative camber into the rear suspension. This much negative camber means the car is going to dart around as it's driven down a straight road.*

Left: *You don't see too many cars with hydro-elastic suspension these days. The British did this on the 1960s Minis. This is a more recent aftermarket version.*
Right: *Here's another Mustang retro design. Ford has a lot to draw on with the Mustang. They also do a very nice job with the retro designs. The tire is a BFG 315/35ZR/17.*

will probably have to pay a pro-rated amount for the new tire, but this should be much less than full price. Pro-rated means that you have to pay for only the tread of tire that has been worn off. Let's say your tire is half worn at the time of the flat. With tires averaging $100 each, your replacement cost would only be $50.

The one question you need to ask is how the company determines the price of the tire when calculating your replacement tire. Will the replacement cost be based on the amount you paid for the tire, or on the list price of the tire? Tires are normally heavily discounted, so ask some questions. It could easily be that a tire on sale will be cheaper than one covered by a pro-rated warranty.

If you travel cross-country, you need a road hazard warranty that allows you to get your tire replaced outside of your local area. This will allow you to travel without worries regarding your tires.

Is a road hazard warranty worth the extra money? I definitely think it is. After driving through construction areas every day for work, I have used my warranty on more than one occasion. It is unfortunate for me that I had tire issues, but when it happened at least I knew I would be covered and not out extra money. A road hazard warranty will let you have peace of mind when you drive through that next nail-filled pothole. So ask about it when you purchase your

next set of tires. Better yet, see if you can get it included in the price of the tires.

WEAR PATTERNS AND YOUR ALIGNMENT

The way your tires wear is a good indicator of what's going on with your car. Abnormal wear patterns are often caused by the need for simple tire maintenance, or for a front-end alignment. Tires should be inspected at least once a month. Learning to read the early warning signs of trouble can prevent wear that shortens tire life or indicates the need for having other parts of the car serviced. Tires should be inspected three ways.

• Look at all four tires for unusual wear patterns

• Run your hand over the tread to detect wear such as feathering

• Check all four tires with a reliable tire pressure gauge

Over Inflation

Excessive wear at the center of the tread indicates that the air pressure in the tire is consistently too high. The tire is riding on the center of the tread and wearing it prematurely. A lot of people fill their tires to the maximum inflation psi found on the tire's sidewall. That's a big mistake. Always check your owner's manual, or the placard on the doorpost. Occasionally, this wear pattern can result from outrageously

Left: *This is a Chip Foose interpretation of the Mustang. Foose has replaced Boyd Codington as king of the bling wheels.* **Right:** *This is the classic smooth look. It's a wonderful solution. The steel wheel is very strong, and lighter than most of the alloy wheels, and the tires are inexpensive. It's possible to look good, be safe, and still have money left in your bank account.*

Left: *A plain Jane Biscayne with some huge tires. The tires are Hoosier radials. Once again this car proves you can have "the look" without going broke.* **Right:** *This look involves more than just tires and wheels. The lights and the bumper area here add to a total approach. Would menacing be the correct term?*

This is what we used to call a reversed rim. In the old days you would cut out the center section and weld it into a new location. It was a way of getting the deep-dish look that was so popular before we had alloy wheel companies.

wide tires on narrow rims. In this case, it's necessary to replace either the tires or the wheels.

Under Inflation

When a tire is under inflated, there's too much contact with the road on the outer edge of the tread area. When this type of wear occurs, and the tire pressure is known to be consistently correct, a bent or worn steering component or the need for wheel alignment could be indicated. Bent steering or idler arms cause incorrect toe-in and abnormal handling characteristics on turns.

Feathering

Feathering is a condition when the edge of the tire develops a slightly rounded edge on one side and a sharp edge on the other. By running your hand over the tire, you can usually feel the sharper edges before you'll be able to see them. The most common cause of feathering is incorrect toe-in setting, which can be cured by setting it correctly. Occasionally, toe-in will be set correctly and this wear pattern still occurs. This is usually due to deteriorated bushings in the front suspension, causing the wheel alignment

to shift as the car moves down the road.

Wear On One Edge

More wear on an inner or outer edge faster than the rest of the tire is due to excessive camber in the front suspension, causing the wheel to lean too much to the inside or outside and putting too much load on one side of the tire. The car may simply need the wheels aligned, but misalignment could be due to sagging springs, worn ball joints, or worn control arm bushings.

Because load has a great effect on alignment, be sure the car is loaded the way it's normally driven when you have the wheels aligned; this is particularly important with independent rear suspension cars.

Cupping

Cups or scalloped dips appearing around the edge of the tread on one side or the other almost always indicate worn suspension parts. Adjustment of wheel alignment alone will seldom cure the problem. Any worn component that connects the wheel to the car (ball joint, wheel bearing, shock absorber, springs, bushings, etc.) can cause this condition.

Occasionally, wheels that are out of balance will wear like this, but wheel imbalance usually shows up as bald spots between the outside edges and center of the tread.

ALIGNMENT

There are two good signs to recognize if your car is properly aligned. First, does the car drive straight down the road? Next, are the tires wearing evenly?

If you're an obsessive person you can measure your tires every six months and keep a record of the wear patterns. Using a tread depth gauge that reads to ½ inch, measure your tires in three places across the face of the tread. The wear should be even all across the tread. If you find uneven wear then it's time for an alignment.

One thing I'm against is aligning a car just to have it aligned. If the car drives straight, and the tires are wearing evenly, just drive the car. Given the state of the repair industry today, there's a good chance that the car will be worse after it's aligned than it was when you took it into the facility.

I get into a more detailed alignment section in Chapter 11 but you do need to think about alignment here. There are a couple of things you should do before you have your car aligned.

First, make sure that the tire pressures are correct. In a perfect world the alignment shop should do this. In the real world they seldom check this. If you really want to check out your car, you can check the suspension for wear. Once again, in the perfect world the alignment shop would check for this. In our imperfect world, shops too often align around problems. Even worse, they too often make up problems that increase the profit on the alignment bay.

Next, take all of the junk out of your car. If you have things such as toolboxes or bags of sand, remove them before you drive to the alignment shop. Extra weight in your car or truck will affect the weight balance of your car, causing one corner to sag more than it should. If you align your vehicle, before removing the junk in your car or truck, the alignment will be off after you clean it out.

Work trucks are a little different. I used to have contractors load their truck the way they usually drove the truck during the week. That way I knew the vehicle was aligned for the normal daily workload.

Tire Balance

Here's a general set of rules for making a decision about when to get your tires balanced.

- When new tires are mounted
- When used tires are installed on existing wheels
- After a flat repair or any time a tire is dismounted and mounted

TIRE ROTATION

I feel I may be the only person in the United States who still rotates tires when it's possible. When it comes to rotation, the first thing is to figure out if the tires and wheels on your car are all the same size. If you have a performance car, you probably have asymmetric tread patterns, or at the very least directional tires. Check for those items. Any of these things mean you just have to give up on a tire rotation.

If by some rare chance you can actually rotate your tires you probably don't have a spare tire. That means you have to figure out how to rotate four wheels. The nice guys at The Tire Rack have figured all of this out for us. This illustration is a little complicated but just figure out which one is your car and then follow the arrows.

Five-Wheel Tire Rotation

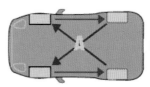

Front Wheel Drive

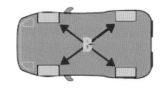

Front Wheel Drive
Rear Wheel Drive

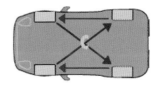

Rear Wheel Drive

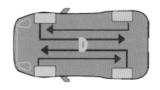

Directional Tires

Five-Wheel Tire Rotation

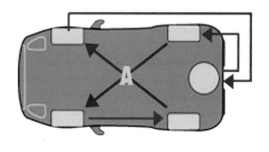

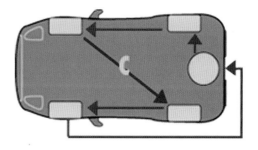

CHAPTER 6
TRUCK TIRES AND WHEELS

For the last few decades it's been all about trucks. Sure we get a new sports car once in a while, but the serious action has been in the truck market. This has happened in both the consumer market and performance aftermarket. One of the problems, however, is that we aren't even sure what a truck is any more. We're pretty sure when it comes to the popular models such as the Ford F-150, Chevy Silverado, and Dodge Ram. Then we have the sport-utility trucks along the lines of the Chevy Avalanche and Explorer Sport Trac. The difference between these different market segments is becoming fuzzier every day.

Then we come to things such as Chrysler's compact PT Cruiser. According to the federal government that's a truck (at least according to the EPA).

Many predict the continuing escalation in gas prices will increase the popularity of compact lifestyle activity vehicles. These are best illustrated by the Pontiac Vibe, Toyota Matrix, and mini-utes such as the Ford Escape, Mazda Tribute, and Honda CRV. In one form or another, light trucks and SUVs are going to be part of the American landscape for some time to come. We just have to figure out what they are. Or, does it really matter?

WHAT'S A TRUCK TIRE?

If you're not really sure of the difference between a truck and a car, let's make this is a little more confusing. Remember in Chapter 2 when we said that a letter P in front of the size stood for passenger tire? So how come when you look at the tires on your new truck or SUV they have a big letter P?

What happened was that the company that designed your truck decided that you really weren't a serious truck person. They figured out that you really cared about ride quality and handling. Hey, for all they know you might even care about how much noise your tires make.

Even though Euro-metric and P-metric tire sizes were designed for cars and station wagons, they've been used a lot lately for light-truck applications. The manufacturers realize that most vans, pickup trucks, and SUVs are really used to carry passengers, not cargo.

These Euro- or P-metric sized tires offer lighter weight, lower rolling resistance, and less aggressive tread designs. All of this makes them better riding, more fuel efficient, and less noisy than your typical truck tire.

Even when the wheel is a one-piece, some wheel designers feel the need to copy the features of a three-piece wheel. The little bolt heads here are fake.

Left: *This is the factory optional wheel. The automotive companies put a lot of effort into their wheels. After all if you have a Hemi under the hood, then your wheels need to be serious.* **Right:** *You'll probably never buy one of these wheels—unless you own a tractor-trailer rig. Nonetheless this is the look that most folks want on their pickup truck.*

There's only one small problem when you use Euro-metric and P-metric sized tires on vans, pickup trucks, and SUVs. If you start using your truck as a real truck, a passenger tire could be a small problem.

Keeping this in mind, the engineers specify Euro- or P-metric sized tires that are rated to carry 10 percent more weight than would be required if they were used on a passenger car. You might think of this as a fudge factor.

Basically they're using passenger car tires on trucks, but using tires that are stronger might be necessary. After all you might actually load something in your truck. The engineers have already accounted for that.

For example, a Euro- or P-metric tire might be designated to carry 2,000 pounds on a car. When this same tire is used on a truck or van it's restricted to carrying 1,820 pounds. This practice provides the vehicle manufacturer with the appropriate tire load capacity for a truck. Keep all of this in mind when you begin to replace your tires. You just can't put any old passenger car tires on a truck.

WHAT ABOUT THE LT TIRE?

LT tires are for people who really don't mind driving a truck. These LT tires are for people who actually need a truck, not a lifestyle statement. LT tires are the little brothers of the heavy-duty tires fitted to 18-wheelers, and use the same basic engineering guidelines regarding load capacity. Because of this, LT-metric sized tires are built strong, and use higher inflation pressures to carry a given load in order to provide the desired safety margin.

Problems begin when you start to replace the tires that came with your new truck. You can't mix LT and P tires. The differences in load capacity and required inflation pressure prohibits mixing the LT tires with Euro or P tires, even if they have equal dimensions. It's all about load capacity, not size.

GOING BIGGER

What makes all of this even more interesting is the growth of two very different trends in aftermarket wheels and tires. One group of people want the plus-size wheels and tires. Keep in mind that we're not talking about a plus one or plus two concept here. We're talking about wheels that are 23 inches and bigger in diameter. Really big tires.

At the very same time the pre-runner style trucks are more popular than ever with their normal diameter wheels and high-profile off-road tires. Different manufacturers are targeting these respective segments with new offerings, providing more choices than ever. As the cynic might say,

Left: This tire was designed for a light truck and is 265 mm wide with the sidewall being 70 percent of that width. It's also a radial tire and mounts on a 17-inch rim. You need to learn how to read sidewalls. It's important.
Above: Here's the load rating for the same tire. Each tire can hold 3,195 pounds. This means that all four tires together can hold over 12,000 pounds. LT tires are designed to hold more than any sane person might carry in their truck.

Hummers have tremendous room for oversize tires and wheels. This is a Mazzi wheel with a Nitto Terra Grabber. Is this look aggressive enough for a Hummer?

you now have even more ways to screw up your truck.

The big trend for sport trucks and SUVs is to install ever-larger diameter wheels. Even the OEMs have gotten into this. The new Chevy Trailblazer offers factory 17-inch wheels, the BMW X-5 has optional 19s, and Ford's Harley-Davidson edition F-150 comes with 20-inch wheels from the factory.

A lot of companies offer up to 23-inch diameter packages for these trucks. Because of the larger diameter of truck tires, the aftermarket industry is able to offer enormous tire and wheel packages that just aren't possible on even the largest passenger cars. Right now the only limitation to having even larger sizes is the ability of tire manufacturers to develop the requisite tires.

Though bigger may be better to the followers of automotive fashion, the plus-size tires and wheels are pushing the limits of practicality. Super-size wheels and tires dramatically increase the unsprung mass of the vehicle, which in turn causes deterioration in ride quality, handling, and braking. These big wheels, and especially the cheap cast wheels, are becoming unreasonably heavy and are contributing to poor handling and really bad ride quality.

You just get to a certain point where the wheel and tire package becomes too heavy and compromises the

Left: This is the standard Ford look. It's a nicely designed wheel with white lettering. You don't always need to look like an off the road vehicle. **Above:** *Here's a case of a passenger tire being used on a truck. Since so many people never use their truck as a truck was meant to be used, the manufacturers are installing a lot of passenger car tires on light-duty pickups and SUVs. There is a considerable amount of difference in ride comfort between a passenger tire and an LT tire.*

vehicle's dynamics, as well as causing the ride, handling, and braking to deteriorate. Factors such as load capacity and vehicle capacity have to be considered.

Some of the higher quality wheel companies are hoping that the next big thing in this market is consumer education. The best way to rate quality is by inquiring about the warranty and how the manufacturer backs up the product. Wouldn't it be nice to know that you can actually get a replacement wheel if something goes wrong in two to four years?

PLUS-SIZING YOUR TRUCK

People often associate plus-sizing with increased cornering response and better traction. These gains often come at the expense of increased ride harshness. In addition, most larger aftermarket wheels are not as durable as original wheels that came with your truck.

A few items of importance if you're considering plus-sizing:
• Make sure that the tires and wheels are approved for use on your vehicle.
• Make sure that the replacement tire has at least the same load-carrying capacity.
• The new wheel and tire combination should be within +/-3 percent of the original tire diameter, or revolutions per mile.

A lot of trucks use 16.5-inch wheels. Some people have placed a 16-inch tire like this on a 16.5-inch wheel. I really don't want to know how they do this but it has happened enough that tire companies actually mold a warning into the sidewall. What makes them think a person who makes such a stupid mistake can even read?

Plus Zero

I've been doing this for years but I just never realized it had a name. Plus zero simply means that you don't change the diameter of the wheels, but you increase the size of the tire. This plus zero choice is almost always the cheapest option available and involves increasing the cross section of the tire

One thing you really should consider in choosing a truck wheel is how easy it is to clean. When you have all of this jewelry on your truck it's a major job just getting the water spots off each week.

while decreasing the aspect ratio of the tire.

For instance, say that the recommended tire for your truck is P195/65R/15. That particular tire has an overall diameter of 25.1 inches. I've figured out that I need to find a 15-inch tire with almost the same diameter but with a larger cross section. A larger cross section usually means a larger tread and a more aggressive look.

When I go to the charts I find a 225/60/15 tire that is

24.7-inches in diameter. That's close enough that I won't be creating any speedometer or ABS problems. I get the more aggressive look for my truck without the expense of new wheels. As far as my truck is concerned these are the same size tire.

Tire Size	Overall Diameter	Revolutions per Mile
P195/65R15	25.1'	829
P225/60R15	24.7'	834

Other Plus-Sizing

Now we get to more expensive options. We're no longer talking about just the tires themselves but the wheels must also be customized to fit these new tires.

For instance, a plus two option for a car with factory tires that are P195/75R/14 may result in P225/60R/16 tires. The increase is 2 inches in rim size but theoretically the overall diameter should stay the same.

Tire Size	Overall Diameter	Revolutions per Mile
P195/75R/14	25.5'	814
P215/60R/16	26.1'	797

Once again these two rather different tires have almost the same diameter and revolutions per mile. At least they're within that 3 percent window. None of this is to say you can actually fit a tire with a 215 mm section width on your truck, but we can say it won't screw up your ABS and speed sensors.

Advantages to Plus-Sizing

The biggest advantage to all of this is how your truck looks. The actual advantages may include a slightly greater handling and cornering ability of the truck, but most of that is

This is a classic truck with some classic American Racing wheels. These wheels are very reasonably priced and blend well with the nostalgia look here. Not everyone needs 19-inch rims. Hell, this truck probably even rides decently with this tire.

Above: Another classic truck with chromed steel wheels. This was all we had until the Chinese discovered how to make really cheap gravity cast alloy wheels that could be dumped in the United States. These wheels are probably stronger than 90 percent of the wheels coming in from China. Right: Here is an all-season LT tire. It's hard to think of Italian (Pirelli) truck tires, but they've been doing a lot of them lately. This is an LT265/70R/17.

a result of the wider tread face and stiffer sidewall of the larger tire size. You could have gotten the same thing by simply buying tires that were stiffer and wider instead of plus-sized.

Plus-sizing is really an option that allows you to customize your truck by installing lower aspect ratio tires on wider and larger diameter rims. A lot of people feel that plus-sizing enhances the look of the vehicle and may improve vehicle performance and handling.

Disadvantages to Plus-Sizing

Plus-sizing past plus one will seldom give you much added performance. Additionally, the tread of the tire is much more likely to wear out more rapidly. A huge disadvantage to plus-sizing is the need for a new set of expensive wheels to match the new tires. Larger tires are also much easier to damage, more susceptible to hydroplaning (riding the surface of the water), and less effective in wet weather. Ride comfort will also have to be sacrificed in order to have the new look.

In addition, plus-sizing may significantly decrease the acceleration, braking, and fuel economy of a vehicle. Even though the overall wheel diameter measured at the tread may stay the same, the combination of moving the heavy wheel outward from the center of the wheel results in a significant increase in rotational mass for each wheel. This increase in offset can result in a measurable increase in the amount of energy necessary to accelerate or decelerate the wheel.

The result of all this is an increase in acceleration times and stopping distances. Like all components in any machine, moving weight from one location to another location where that weight has to be moved through a larger distance will result in reduced response times. Any change of this manner will have a detrimental overall effect on a vehicle's performance.

Plus-sizing also doesn't enhance the value of the vehicle; in many cases it diminishes value, since a new set of wheels means the vehicle is no longer original. Most used car buyers prefer a stock truck when they go shopping. The market for a personalized truck is usually very small. You may love your custom touches but that doesn't mean everyone will love them.

The following are some really important things that need to be considered in every plus-sizing action. Think of these as basic rules. You can violate all rules, but there will be consequences. Not necessarily good ones, either.

LOAD CAPACITY

The capacity of the new tire to handle a load must be equal to or greater than the load capacity of the original equipment tire. Don't ever put a tire on your truck or SUV that has a load rating less than the original tire.

The best system for checking this is reading the vehicle door placard or owner's manual for the load index specified for the original equipment tire. Don't count on your current tires being correct. A lot of us drive older vehicles and a previous owner may have put smaller tires on the truck. Never overestimate the intelligence of a previous owner.

Load Index

The load index is found on the side of every P-metric tire. Let's use this as an example: P195/60R/15 87S. The load index (87) is the tire size's assigned numerical value for relative load carrying capabilities. In the case of our example, the 87 identifies the tire's ability to carry approximately 1,201 pounds.

The higher the tire's load index number, the greater its load carrying capacity. Just to make this simple you first need to find out what the original Load Index was and then you need to select a tire with the same or larger number.

Load Index	Pounds	Load Index	Pounds
71	761	91	1356
72	783	92	1389
73	805	93	1433
74	827	94	1477
75	853	95	1521
76	882	96	1565
77	908	97	1609
78	937	98	1653
79	963	99	1709
80	992	100	1764
81	1019	101	1819
82	1047	102	1874
83	1074	103	1929
84	1102	104	1984
85	1135	105	2039
86	1168	106	2094
87	1201	107	2149
88	1235	108	2205
89	1279	109	2271
90	1323	110	2337

If your new tire has a higher load index than the original tire, you've actually increased the load capacity of the vehicle, or at least the ability of the tires to handle the load. Keep in mind that the springs and frame are still the original from the factory. Just because you have tires with increased load capacity doesn't mean you can overload your truck. It just means you have safe tires on your truck.

A tire with a load index equal to that of the original equipment tire indicates an equivalent load capacity. A tire with a lower load index than the original equipment tire indicates the tire does not equal the load capacity of the original—not a good idea.

This is what I call the Peterbilt look. It's one step up from the factory wheels and tires, yet at the same time you get some degree of ride comfort, and not a lot of noise. The wheel design mimics the big rig look.

Load Range and Ply Rating

You already know that every tire is designed to support a certain amount of weight. Now we get to a little complication with real trucks, or at least with real truck tires. Truck tires are frequently marked with a ply rating and equivalent load range. These markings are used to identify the load and inflation limits of that particular tire when used in a specific type of service.

Ply ratings: This is an older method of rating load capacity; these are listed as 4-ply, 6-ply, 8-ply, etc.

Load ratings: The current method of rating a tire's load-carrying capacity is denoted by letters (B, C, D, E, etc.).

	Load Range	Ply Rating	Load Pressure (PSI)
LT-metric	B	4	35
LT-numeric	C	6	50
Flotation LT	D	8	65
	E	10	80
	F	12	95

INFLATION PRESSURE

You should never use a tire inflation pressure lower than the original equipment specification. The recommended inflation pressure for the vehicle's original equipment tires is normally located on the door placard, inside the fuel filler

Here's a street truck that mimics the off-road look. I seriously doubt that this truck sees deep mud, but the owner loves the look so much that he's willing to sacrifice ride comfort and highway handling ability. You just make your choices and pay your money.

This is a stock Tacoma. This is a pretty aggressive package right from the factory. The tire is a Bridgestone Dueler H/T that emphasizes a smooth quiet ride. They used a small block tread design with extremely high tread. It's also an S-rated tire, which means it's been tested to 112 miles per hour. The only problem is that as the tires wear you'll experience an increase in tread noise. Then again you always get that with a block design.

flap, or in the owner's manual. Never use tire inflation pressures below the original equipment manufacturer's recommendations.

Always maintain the relative tire inflation pressure difference between the front and rear axle tires as specified by the manufacturer of the truck. The tire pressure relationship between axles must be maintained so vehicle handling and stability is not adversely affected.

Using the wrong tire pressure causes rapid and/or irregular tire wear, reduced tire life, poor fuel econ-omy, and eventual tire failure.

Never exceed the maximum tire inflation pressure as stated on the tire sidewall.

SPEED RATING

If you install new tires, the speed rating for the new ones must be equal to or greater than the tires that were installed at the factory. That sounds easy but you would be surprised at how many people violate this rule just to get that special look on their truck. Or, to keep the VISA bill a little lower.

If the vehicle is as big as a Hummer H2, then you need some really big rims.

Left: We're back to the classic wheel look with some white letters. The best part of this combination is the reasonable cost. You'll never wow them on cruise night but the combination is a cost-effective solution. **Right:** The Michelin X started the whole radial thing many decades ago. Now it's hard to think of this tire as being exotic.

The speed ratings for tires are identified by means of a speed symbol. The speed symbol indicates the speed category at which the tire can carry a load corresponding to its load index. The speed symbol is located on the tire sidewall after the size designation.

The speed rating is an alphabetic code (P205/55ZR/16 89 Y). In this example it's the letter Y. That means the tire has been tested to 186 miles an hour with no problems.

ROLLING CIRCUMFERENCE

The rolling circumference of the original equipment tires is a big deal. If the original equipment tires are replaced with tires that have a rolling circumference different from the original tires it could affect the speedometer calibration, anti-lock brake systems (ABS), and stability control systems.

The original equipment rolling circumference should be maintained as closely as possible. Close in this case means no more than a 3 percent difference. You can always look this infor-

90

This is an LT tire which means the Load Range is expressed differently from a passenger car tire. A light truck tire's ply rating and/or load range doesn't count the actual number of body plies found inside the tire, but indicates an equivalent strength based on earlier bias-ply tires.

	Load Range	Ply Rating	Maximum Load Pressure (PSI)
P-Metric Tire	Standard Load	-	35
	Extra Load	-	41
	B	4	35
Light Truck	C	6	50
	D	8	65
	E	10	80
	F	12	95

mation up on the web (www.thetirerack.com), or see if the local tire store can find it for you. It's usually easier to use the Internet.

An alternative to the rolling circumference is the revolutions per mile, or even the tire diameter information provided in a product guide or technical data book. Once again I find The Tire Rack charts easiest to use.

BODY AND CHASSIS CLEARANCE

If you're replacing your tires and wheels with ones that are different from the original equipment specifications you need to do a lot of checking. All of the clearances between the tires and the vehicle's components need to be checked, including the full suspension travel for both front and rear applications and the full range of motion for the steer tires.

Make sure you include clearance for tire growth and deflection under load and cornering conditions. Check everything that could come into contact with your new tires and wheels. That includes the brake hoses and all of the steering components.

LIGHT TRUCK TIRE SIDEWALL INFORMATION

Most of the markings on a light truck tire sidewall have the same meaning as those on passenger tire sidewalls. The following additional markings apply only to light truck tires.

What follows below is for real truck tires. This is all very similar to the numeric system that's used for cars. The system lists the section width in inches, the construction type, and the rim diameter in inches. The LT for the light truck designation is then placed at the end of the numeric sequence.

This is a Goodyear Wrangler HP P265/70R/17. This tire is really a passenger car tire that's used on a lot of trucks. One of the most common installations is on the Cadillac Escalade. You get a big tire with ride comfort.

DUAL REAR TIRES

This is a special case. Trucks with dual rear wheels are special. The basic rule here is that you can't change tire sizes. Whatever came installed on your dualie is what you need to get when it's time for replacement. Just about everything on these trucks are unique. The axles are special and the wheels are special.

The wheels on dualies feature extreme offsets that allow them to be installed center-to-center on the rear axle. The inner wheel uses an extreme positive offset, which allows the tire and wheel to be placed just like normal, with its backside going over the axle.

The outer wheel uses extreme negative offset and is installed on the axle with its center against the inner wheel's center. The back of the wheel is actually facing outward.

All of this means the wheel width and offset are carefully engineered for the vehicle and the selected tire size. This allows them to match the vehicle's requirements while assuring sufficient clearance is maintained between the pairs of tires on the rear axle so their sidewalls don't rub each other under maximum load when cornering or running over large bumps.

While both front and rear axles are heavy-duty with eight-bolt hubs, the front axles are longer than normal to accommodate wheels with extreme positive offset. The rear axles are sized to fit a pair of tires and wheels on each side between the vehicle's frame to the inside and its flared fender on the outside.

Considering all of this, it's obvious why you can't put bigger tires on the rear axle of a dualie truck. If you put bigger tires on those rear wheels then you're going to have a huge rubbing issue. The tire sidewalls will actually hit each other.

All four tires should be the same size and be the same brand. Even a slight difference in diameter means that your truck is only riding on three, or maybe even two, tires.

*Left: Dual rear tires need to be exactly the same. You simply can't have a variation in diameter. That means you need to replace all four rear tires at the same time. This way you can be assured that the tires will all be the exact same diameter, and won't rub against each other. **Right:** Even trucks get into the old Torq-Thrust wheels. This wheel is perfect for this Ranchero pickup.*

Light Truck Metric Sizing System

This label is very similar to the P-metric system used on passenger cars except the P is replaced with the LT light truck designation. Keep in mind, though, that the LT-metric light truck tires and P-metric passenger car tires differ in construction.

Light Truck High Flotation System

This seems a little confusing at first but you just have to keep in mind that the first number is the diameter of the tire. The rest of the numbers follow the normal pattern. You'll find this system in use for a lot of the trail and mud tires found on full-size 4x4 vehicles.

This designation evolved during the mid 1970s as lower aspect ratio tires became popular.

Here's a graphic comparison of the three different tire descriptions.

	Size Designation	Actual Dimensions in Inches
High Flotation	30x9.5R15	29.8x9.6
LT-Metric	LT235/75R15	29.2x9.3
LT-Numeric	7.00R15LT	30.3x8.1

As the size increases, Flotation tires will have a wider overall width than the LT-Metric and LT-Numeric tires. Another big difference is that flotation tires typically require wider wheels than the LT-Metric and LT-Numeric tires. Make sure you ask a lot of questions and do some research before you switch to a flotation tire.

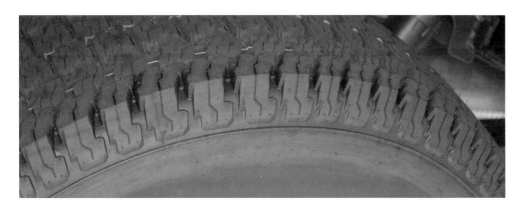

This is a great example of a tire that is great for construction sites and some fire trail use. At the same time it's a great all-round tire. It's a Goodyear in a light truck size of LT 275/65R18.

I think of this as the non-truck truck. You probably won't ever see this truck at the Home Depot loading up on sheet rock. You will though see it on a cruise night. The tire and wheel are designed just for that.

CHAPTER 7
OFF-ROAD TIRES AND WHEELS

Mud is mud and rocks are rocks. How much difference does the type of wheel and tire really make? Actually, a lot. Getting stuck in the woods without your cell phone is only one of your possible problems. You can have your tires jump off the wheel or you can rip a hole in the sidewall. You can even break a wheel. The good news is that all of this can be avoided (well, at least minimized) if you buy the right wheels and tires.

Even though it may seem like little is new in off-road wheels and tires, everyone just keeps pushing the envelope, producing stronger wheels and tires at an increasingly lower cost. Furthermore, trick-forged wheels and bead-lock wheels previously found only on high dollar race trucks and purpose-built 4x4s are becoming increasingly common on daily drivers and weekend warriors alike.

Style? The aftermarket has a slew of styles to fit anyone's taste, from the basic to the outlandish. In fact, I think some of these wheels were designed for people with no taste at all. Sorry about that but you know what I mean. Even worse, some of them have no strength. But they're really cheap. As if that makes up for everything.

STRONG WHEELS ARE GOOD WHEELS

The most critical item for an off-road wheel is strength. Pretty just doesn't cut it 50 miles back into a fire trail. The way a wheel is manufactured is still the best indication of strength.

Almost all steel wheels are two-piece in design. (Three-piece steel wheels are available on the aftermarket but they're just not that common anymore.) Steel wheels use an inner section that's stamped on a press and then welded to a formed steel rim. Steel wheels are strong and they're inexpensive. They are very practical in the back woods since they won't easily break. Yet most people don't consider them because they lack presence. They're just too utilitarian

Most aluminum, or alloy wheels (both OE and aftermarket) are either one-piece or two-piece construction. Remember that a one-piece wheel is just that: a single piece of aluminum shaped (usually by casting) into a wheel.

The strongest overall aluminum wheel is a forged version. During forging, a billet (piece) of aluminum is forced (forged) into the shape of a wheel by a huge press using tremendous pressure. Forged wheels are usually a two-piece

When you get to tires such as this Mickey Thompson, notice how the tread actually wraps halfway down the sidewall. This makes this tire good in the mud.

design. In the two-piece design the center section is welded to an outer rim.

The alloy wheels often have weight advantage. The reduced weight of an alloy wheel gives you better mileage and it will also create less of a strain on the bearings and other parts. On the other hand they're going to cost you more. Also, alloy wheels can break if they get a hit from a rock and can be difficult to fix in the wilderness. Steel wheels will bend and can be hammered back to some semblance of a shape. At the very least they can be bent back far enough to hold air.

In the off-road world, wheel weight is secondary to strength. Wheel weight simply isn't much of a factor. With people running between 35- and 40-inch-tall tires, the weight of the wheels isn't an issue because the tires are so big. You could take five pounds out of a wheel, but most people are never going to feel the difference. If you made one that weighed only 10 pounds instead of 38, then it would make a difference, but a wheel that light might not even stay on the vehicle.

Hub-Centric Wheels

Most of the new off-road wheels are hub-centric. With a hub-centric wheel, the large center hole is precisely sized and has a chamfer where it meets the wheel hub. When the wheel is installed and the lug nuts are tightened, the raised center section of the hub fits tightly into the chamfered hole on the wheel.

With a hub-centric design, the wheel studs don't have to

BEAD PROTECTION

If you've been out playing in the mud, you've probably already figured out that the bead areas of a tire and wheel are always potential trouble areas. Because of the location of the wheel and tire beads, they're subject to damage from encounters with rocks and tough terrain. Bead-lock wheels and wheels with bead-reinforcement rings are two methods for keeping the tire and wheel intact.

Another small but effective shield against damage to a wheel's outer bead lip is BFGoodrich's Rim Protector, used on BFG's Radial Mud-Terrain. Essentially, a thick piece of rubber that extends outward (laterally) away from the wheel and tire bead area, the Rim Protector provides an extra cushion against the damage inflicted by rocks and other solid obstacles. While it's hardly high-tech, the BFG Rim Protector is simple, reliable, and functional.

support the vehicle's weight. The wheel is supported in the horizontal plane by the precision fit between the hub and the wheel's center bore.

On a lug-centric wheel, the wheel studs and lug nuts perform double-duty as they pull the wheel into contact with the wheel hub and also provide support to the wheel in the vertical plane. In other words, the wheel studs and lug nuts support the entire weight of the vehicle. The only reason for this design is to save on production costs.

This is huge. This is a bias-ply tire designed for mud. The bias-ply construction allows the tire to move around in a bog better than a radial could. This same movement in a street tire might not be desirable, but it's exactly what you want in a mud tire.

Left: *Remember that mud tires have a directional tread.* **Above:** *This is expensive. Remote reservoir shocks are designed to increase the oil capacity. This increase in oil capacity prevents the shock oil from overheating and breaking down. When shock oil overheats, the damping effect of the shock is lessened. To ensure consistent handling and performance a reservoir is an excellent feature. Heavier trucks can use more than one shock per corner. In this case the owner used some nice brackets to mount the reservoirs right alongside the shocks.*

BEYOND YOUR BASIC TIRE

Choices abound for off-road tires. You have to be very honest about how you intend to use your vehicle. A great mud tire is going to make a lot of noise on the highway. A great highway tire might get you stuck in the swamp. Sure tires are better than they used to be, but you still have to make choices.

Every type and style of off-road tire derives its performance from its fundamental design and construction. Similar-appearing tires can vary widely in the number of plies, the depth and style of the tread, the basic carcass construction, and whether or not the sidewall is designed to provide traction under certain conditions. That said, here's an overview of what makes a rugged, traction-grabbing off-road tire.

Choose the Tire First

You should select the tire before you decide on the wheel. Let the tire dictate the wheel, rather than the other way around. For instance if you drive on the street, with an occasional foray down a fire trail, you probably don't need a huge tire. You might want one of the all-terrain tires that can be used on a normal wheel (whatever that is).

When it comes to your truck or Jeep, the tire is going to make a lot more difference than the wheel. The only job of the wheel is to hold the tire. Not many people have been stuck in the woods because of the wheel. Unless, that is, if they bought their wheels based on price.

Bias-Ply vs. Radial

If you spend most of your time driving on the road, a radial tire is usually the best choice. The shock absorbing nature of the radial tire sidewall will give you a smooth ride. The flat tread area also provides good directional stability and traction.

For serious off-road driving, though, the bias-ply tire is a stronger tire. The bias construction tolerates twisting and bending from rocks and roots. Since the sidewall is as strong as the rest of the body, it can take lateral loads from rocks and roots without splitting.

Bias-ply tires can survive abuse that would destroy a radial. The radial's sidewall plies don't reinforce each other, making them very vulnerable to splitting from twisting, bending, and side loads. The bias-ply tire can use extremely

aggressive treads for excellent traction. Sidewall tread blocks can help protect the sidewall and also add traction to climb out of ruts and up rocks.

For more moderate off-roading, a case can be made for either design. While the radial has the disadvantages just discussed, the radial's flexibility gives it a smoother ride. Bias-ply tires are the clear choice for off-roading in conditions where sidewall strength, larger tread lugs, and sidewall traction are of paramount concern. Radials with their longer tread life, smoother ride, and good control are the best for on-road driving.

Many people swear by one or the other. As with most things, there isn't a clear-cut superiority of one over another. Most serious off-road tire makers produce both designs to satisfy different needs. Remember that bias-ply tires served the industry for many years before the invention of the radial, and the technology has improved the bias tire dramatically. On the flip side, radials were invented for a reason. The most important question though is where do you really drive your Jeep or truck.

Narrow vs. Wide

Wide tires are used where flotation and stability are desired. The tall narrow tires will have greater contact pressure, so when crossing a sensitive area such as a muddy track, the tire will want to dig down until traction is found as opposed to floating on top.

Narrow tires provide less stability on the road and on cambered trails. In addition, a taller, narrow tire's side-walls deflect more under severe turning forces, causing the inside of the tire's contact patch to lift from the road, increasing the chance of a skid, or loss of control.

If you drive in mud or snow, the last thing in the world you want is a wide tire. Basically wide tires make the footprint larger, which results in less penetration into the soil and therefore less traction. That means more skidding and the chance of getting stuck.

Even the off-road wheels are getting into the black trend. The tire is a Mickey Thompson light truck tire.

BEAD LOCKS AND POSITIVE TIRE RETENTION

The theory behind a bead lock lies in its mechanical retention of a tire. On a non-bead-lock wheel, the tire's bead is retained on the wheel by the wheel's bead seat (the area between the outer wheel lip and the raised inner hump) and the rubber-wrapped steel cables found within the tire's bead. Most important, the tire stays in place because of the tire's internal air pressure.

Off-road folks lower the tire pressure to get maximum traction. Now think about what I said up above. The air pressure holds the tire in place. Take the air pressure away and you have a problem. If you don't have air pressure, then the tire can move around on the wheel.

When the tire pressure gets down to less than 15 psi, the tire may move laterally on the wheel's bead seat, resulting in a total loss of air pressure. At that point the tire bead can slip right off the wheel. At the very least you'll have a flat tire.

Bead locks eliminate the tire's bead movement through the use of clamping pressure. A standard bead lock is designed to clamp the tire bead between an outer and an inner ring. The inner ring may be welded onto a standard wheel increasing wheel width by anywhere from 1½ to 2 inches or may be formed as part of the wheel when the wheel is made in the factory. The outer ring is then bolted onto the inner ring with the bead clamped between them. Anywhere between 16 and 32 bolts at around 10 lbs-ft of torque are used around the circumference of the wheel to keep the clamp tight.

These rings and bolts can cause problems with balancing the wheel and tire because all the added weight is on one side. Solve one problem and create another one. Oh well.

It's important to note that most standard bead locks clamp only the outside bead. This is fine in most cases because the outside bead is the side that comes unseated while off-roading. With the tire thus retained, lateral bead movement is eliminated, and the tire will remain on the rim even with zero air pressure in the tire.

Actually all of this is a little academic anyway since bead locks are illegal in most states.. Most 4x4 and off-road stores won't sell them and you have to get them from a mail order company. The main point here is that you need to understand the reason people use bead locks, and what might happen if you let too much air out of your tires.

This is illegal in a lot of states. A lot of states require that the fender cover the tread of the tire. Your local 4x4 shop will be very familiar with the law. Just because you see trucks like this around town doesn't mean the police can't give you a ticket.

The mantra is:
- Sand or rock = wide tires for flotation and protection from flats
- Mud and snow = skinny tires for penetration and traction

Taller Is Better

A taller tire gives you more clearance under the differential and chassis. A wider tire (or change in tread pattern) gives you more traction. Four-wheelers frequently put 35-inch tires on their trucks because most trails recommend this size.

If you choose to put tires larger than 31 inches on your rig, then you'll most likely have to lift your vehicle. In that

Above: This is the Super Swamper by Interco Tire Corporation (www.intercotire.com). This tire uses short, intermediate, and long massive lugs to bite quickly and to self-clean. Interco is very vocal about the amount of air that should be in its tires. The company points out that two things support the weight of a vehicle. First, the volume of air; second, the air pressure. With big tires the large volume of air in the tire will support the truck but the tire will not be stable with low pressures. The tire will look okay, but when driven on the highway it'll wiggle and squirm. This isn't important when running off road because you don't go very fast, plus the ground is softer than the tire. When you get back on the highway you should bring the pressure back up again. Big tires will almost always look like they have enough air when, actually, they may not. *Left:* This big block raises the suspension, and the body, of the truck.

case, you'll need to be aware of the lift laws in your state. A large number of states have very strict laws regarding your bumpers. It's also important to keep in mind that lifting your vehicle also raises its center of gravity, thus increasing your chances for rollover.

Whenever you go to a larger tire size you should consider changing your front- and rear-end gear ratios to offset the size. Remember that the diameter of your tire is part of the total gear ratio equation. A good, local 4x4 store should be able to help you work out all of the math involved.

Tread Patterns

Looking at the various tread designs available on the aftermarket will confuse even the best-informed enthusiast. Each manufacturer has its own unique tread style, and each design is supported with plenty of reasons why it's the best for producing traction. Short of testing all the tires on the

market, you can make a tread decision based on your projected use, what sizes are available, and how much these tires are going to cost.

After checking the available balance on your VISA, you should decide which of the three different tread styles to consider. The most aggressive is the mud-terrain, followed by what can best be called an all-terrain tread. Then comes the tire some call a trail tread.

A lot of people feel you should have the most aggressive tire you can find. The thinking is that you should always be prepared for the worst. When things get muddy, an all-terrain tread won't cut it and you'll get stuck. Then ask yourself if you can stand driving to work every day with the whine of an aggressive tire tread. How often do you really go off road?

The opposing view is that all-terrain tires have become better in various types of terrain and are even useful in light-

Left: This wheel is fabricated out of sheets of steel. When you realize it's 24 inches from the outside of the wheel to where the wheel bolts to the hub, you get the idea. Right: I've always believed that tread design is an art form. It seems to be most apparent in the off-road tires. We all know what the tread has to do, but every designer has his or her own opinion about how best to do it.

Left: A 36-inch tire is large, and 15.5 inches is rather wide. This particular tire fits on a 20-inch rim. I'm a little amused that it's called an all-season tire. It seems that the term all-season has lost all meaning and is simply a marketing term. Right: I think off-road people will debate the effectiveness of the radial vs. the bias-ply tire for the next two decades.

Having the tread wrap down onto the sidewall provides you with a tremendous increase in traction. This tread area extends almost halfway down the sidewall.

to-moderate amounts of mud. All-terrain tires are a compromise no doubt, but with a locker or limited-slip in the rear axle and an air locker in the front differential, an all-terrain tire 4x4 can make serious headway across rugged terrain.

The choice of tread pattern is important in your new tire decision-making process. Tread pattern should be chosen based on the intended use of your off-road excursions. The most popular tread pattern for all-around off-road use is a mud terrain pattern. On the other hand, most stores sell a lot of trail tires. As with all tires it's a series of tradeoffs. No tire does everything well.

Trail Treads: A variety of manufacturers offers what is called a trail tire, or something near that. These are tires designed for use on light trucks or sport utility vehicles that see most

Left: One of the real problems in the service field is that there are both 16-inch and 16.5-inch wheels. As difficult as it may be to understand, people get the wrong tires put on these wheels. Here the tire company is taking no chances. *Right:* These are some huge tread lugs. The space between the lugs is called a void. This means the tire will actually throw off the mud as it gets into the tread.

The tire company has molded this safety warning into the sidewall. It's interesting that the company calls this an all-season tire. It's gotten to the point where the all-season category has lost all meaning.

of their use on the street. They will generally be quieter, get better gas mileage, and last longer than either of the other off-road patterns.

The tread patterns are designed to provide comfort and performance on the street that can sometimes compromise serious off-road capability. I personally would not recommend them for anything other than light off-road use such as dirt, or unpaved roads or trails where you are unlikely to encounter mud, significant rocks, or other unpleasant conditions.

All-Terrain Tires: The all-terrain tire generally has an interlocked tread pattern with siping (small cuts) on the tread blocks. The voids in these tires are also generally much smaller than those on tires designed for use in the mud. The

Another view of the tread placed on the sidewall.

Left: Here you can see the huge voids in the tire tread. This is what makes this tire so effective in the mud. On the other hand, this tire has very little tread that actually comes into contact with the pavement. This tire could make for very exciting times on wet pavement. Right: The interesting thing with this tire is that it's almost as if it's been siped in the mold. The little vertical cracks are very much like siping. In fact, it is siping.

Wheel spacers have a place. They can also put some very unique stress on your wheels. This spacer actually bolts to the hub and then the wheel is bolted to the spacer.

dense pattern of blocks and smaller voids make these tires quieter on the street than a mud tire. This pattern also increases the surface area of the tread, which gives the tire improved flotation on surfaces such as light powdery snow or sand. The increased siping can be important in snow where the number of edges (even very small edges) provides the bite into the snow.

In addition, the multi-faceted tread blocks deliver traction from any direction on dirt, sand, and gravel; and provide handling, acceleration, and stopping ability. The lugs on the shoulder of the tire and the pockets between each lug foster good off-road steering response and traction. This is a tire for dirt trails, rocky trails, shallow mud, and moderate to heavy snow, yet it remains fairly civilized for highway use. The downside is that the smaller voids cannot clean themselves of packed mud and slush as easily as the larger voids on mud tires do. When these small voids fill up with mud, the tire loses much of its bite and

Left: This is a huge forged-aluminum wheel. This is a good example where the tire was selected first then the owner looked around for a very strong wheel. That's not the best sequence. *Right:* This is where it all started: An old jeep with some oversize tires and some cheap steel wheels. This is a two-piece steel wheel. The center section was stamped out and then welded to the rim. These are very strong wheels, and, even better, if you bend this wheel out in the woods you can pound it back into shape with a small sledgehammer.

traction is lost.

All of this is accomplished by using a tread pattern design where the lugs are tighter together than a more aggressive mud tire's tread. The result is usually a quieter ride on the street than what you might get from a true mud tire. Quite simply, a less aggressive tread pattern will make less noise. When compared to a street tire, all-terrain tires are going to produce quite a bit more noise.

All-terrain tires are really a compromise. All-terrain tires are an attempt to offer good performance both on road as well as off road. The all-terrain tread is designed to perform well under a variety of conditions found off road while still offering acceptable on-highway performance. The all-terrain tire is for the daily driver who occasionally ventures onto the trails. This is a street tire that gives you the look without the nasty noise.

The benefit of all-terrain tires is that they perform well

on a variety of terrains such as rocks, sand, and somewhat decent in the mud while still offering decent traction on the paved road.

Mud Tires: The mud-terrain or mud tire pattern is easily recognized by the large lugs on the tire with huge spaces, or voids, between the lugs. The goal of this tire is to bite into loose or muddy surface areas for maximum traction and propel the vehicle forward. The very large opening between the lugs helps make the tire self-cleaning. The mud is compressed as the tire gets a grip and then expelled as the tire rolls on. Tires with smaller grooves allow the mud to pack into the tread and not be expelled. Wide grooves also help the tire perform well on loose shale and rocks.

These tires are also very popular for rock crawling as the large lugs can provide a way of gripping and pulling the tires up and over irregular rocky edges where a smoother pattern

Left: You won't have too much luck pounding this wheel back into shape if you hit something in the woods. Then again, this wheel may be too perfect to ever see a real trail. **Right:** This is a light truck tire that has an all-season tread. I think almost everything today is being called all-season. The tire is an LT265/75R/16. The height of this tire makes it a great choice for trail riding.

This is all about the look; this truck is just too perfect to have spent much time in the mud.

Left: Once again we have a great trail tire, but a pretty bad tire for the rain. You just can't have one tire do it all. *Right:* Fender extensions not only protect the paint on the sides of your truck, they'll keep water from splashing all over other people as you drive down the highway.

would just spin. The biggest disadvantage of these patterns is that they run rough and loud on the highway. You can reduce this slightly by selecting a tire with irregular or asymmetric spacing of the lugs and voids to reduce harmonic vibration at highway speeds.

There are also situations such as cold powder snow or sand where an all-terrain pattern would be better. While the all-terrain pattern's improved flotation and additional siping may be an advantage in absolutely dry powder or packed snow, the mud terrain may be the wiser choice if the snow or underlying terrain is slushy or muddy. In these cases the all-terrain pattern will become packed with mud and stuck where a mud-terrain pattern would self-clean and plow on through.

Mud-terrain tires are designed to perform in the mud but also perform quite well in conditions such as on the rocks, in deep snow, as well as in loose gravel. They work surprisingly well in the softer, constantly changing terrain of wooded trails. This is because mud tires are usually designed with a softer compound, which when coupled

This is a good example of an all-purpose off-road tread. The voids, or spaces, between the tread blocks are small enough that you have some contact on the pavement. At the same time, the tread is aggressive enough to get you down the average fire trail, and across hard-packed sand. This tire won't be too noisy in the beginning but as the tread blocks wear the noise will increase. This block-type of tread design gets noisy as the block wears on the leading edge.

with the wider gaps between the lugs (voids) can grab on to anything it can hook one of its edges around, especially when the tire is aired down.

The drawback of the mud tire is that it performs poorly on the highway. They're especially bad in the rain where the wide lug pattern results in hardly any contact between the tire and the road. Even worse, they can be downright dangerous in icy conditions. Only a small patch of tire touch-ing the pavement at any given moment (the contact area) is solely responsible for keeping your vehicle under control. These huge tires may have contact area that's only about 6 square inches in size.

Mud tires tend to wear far quicker than an all-terrain or a street tire. The highway noise level will increase greatly after they wear down with use. Maybe the biggest problem with the aggressive tread of the mud tires is that they're noisy. Really noisy. This is a case where you might want to actually consider a second set of tires if you use your 4x4 for daily commuting.

Once you go to a mud tire you've really compromised the truck as a street vehicle. By optimizing it for the mud you've significantly reduced the ability of the truck to be used on pavement. That shouldn't surprise you. Life is full of compromises.

SOME OTHER THINGS TO CONSIDER

Tire Pressures: Really low tire pressure will increase your traction out on the trail. That's the good part. The downside of this low pressure is that your speed is limited. You have to be careful to make sure the bead of the tire stays attached to the wheel. The bead found on most wheels is not deep enough to keep the tire on the wheel if the pressure is lowered too far.

Also, keep in mind that lower tire pressure will also make the sidewalls of the tire more vulnerable to damage. I'm sure you've noticed that large bulge on the bottom of your tire when you get down to 15 pounds of pressure. A final caution is to remember that when you lower the tire pressures you're decreasing your ground clearance several inches since you're reducing the working diameter of the tire.

Lowering the air pressure in you tires, though, is still the easiest and cheapest method of increasing your off-road performance. While it's common to lower tire pressure if you're going off-road, don't reduce your tire pressure when on the highway. Also, keep in mind that you're going to have to drive home on a regular highway. Make an air tank part of your gear.

SIPING

This is a process of cutting thin slits across a rubber surface to improve traction in wet or icy conditions. Siping was invented and patented by John Sipe in the 1920s. Sipe worked in a slaughterhouse and grew tired of slipping on the wet floors. He found that cutting slits in the tread on the bottoms of his shoes provided better traction than the uncut tread.

The process was not applied to vehicle tires on a large scale until the 1950s. As is often the case, there are compromises. Winter tires, and "mud and snow" tires, may have thousands of sipes and give good traction. But, they may feel "squirmy" on a warm, dry road.

Large sipes are usually built into the tread during manufacturing. Sipes may also be cut into the tread at a later date, called microsiping. Bandag, a major retreading company, developed a machine for micro siping that places a curved knife blade at a slight angle on a rotating drum. The knife makes a series of diagonal cuts across the tread. For improved traction, the tire may be siped twice, leaving diamond-shaped blocks.

Microsiping can dramatically improve tire traction in rain and snow. However, these microsiped tires will also have increased road noise and tire wear when operated on dry surfaces.

Both Bridgestone and Michelin sell snow tires that are siped at the factory, while Saf-Tee Siping and Grooving sell machines that can sipe most standard vehicle tires.

Keep in mind that most tire manufacturers really don't like siping, especially the handmade siping. They feel that rough rocks will actually take chunks out of the tire between the sipes. Secondly, they feel that small rocks can get wedged into the sipes, giving you extra noise and tire wear when you're back on the bitumen. Be aware that siping the tires can void the manufacturer's warranty.

SIZES AND DIAMETERS

Approx. Tire Diameter (in Inches)	P-metric and European Metric			LT-metric		Light Truck Flotation	Light Truck Numeric
	75-series and Higher	70- and 65-series	60-series and Lower	85-series	75-series and Lower		
34-1/2						35X12.50R15LT	
33-1/2				LT255/85R16			
33					LT285/75R16		
32-1/2						33X12.50R16.5LT	
					33X12.50R15LT		
31-1/2		P275/70R16		LT235/85R16	LT265/75R16	32X11.50R15LT	7.50R16
30-1/2	P265/75R15	265/70R16	285/60R17	LT215/85R16	LT285/60R17	31X10.50R16.5LT	9.50R16.5LT
				LT245/75R16	31X11.50R15LT		
				LT325/60R15	31X10.50R15LT		
30		P2550/70R16	P275/60R17				
29-1/2		P245/70R16	265/60R17		LT225/75R16	30X9.50R15LT	8.75R16.5LT
						7.00R15	
29	205R16	255/65R16	255/55R18		LT235/75R15		
	205/80R16	P235/70R16	255/60R17				
	P235/75R15	P255/70R15					
28-1/2	P225/75R15	P225/70R16			LT225/75R15	29X9.50R15LT	8.00R16.5LT
	P245/70R15						
28		215/70R16	P255/55R17				
	P275/60R15						
27-1/2	P215/75R15	P225/70R15			LT215/75R15		
27	P205/75R15	P215/65R16	255/50R17		LT205/75R15		
		P305/50R15					
		P255/60R15					
26-1/2	P195/75R15	P225/70R14	P295/50R15		LT195/75R15	27X8.50R14LT	
		P245/60R15					
26	P205/75R14	P215/65R15	P235/60R15				
	185R14	P215/70R14					
25-1/2	P195/75R14	P205/70R14	P225/60R15				

Courtesy of The Tire Rack

CHAPTER 8
DETAILING TIRES AND WHEELS

Tires make a visual statement about who you are. Even if you never enter a car show, you still make that statement. You make a statement every day as you drive to work. You make that statement when you just stop at a car show on the weekend.

Think of your tires and wheels as your shoes. You wouldn't wear scuffed-up loafers with your new Ralph Lauren suit. If you go to Banana Republic you certainly wouldn't wear cheap dirty shoes from K-Mart. All of this goes for your car as well. You just spent a bunch of money on tires and wheels. You're looking good. Now how do you keep that look?

TIRE CARE

Ozone and ultraviolet light are trying to destroy your tires. They attack the long hydrocarbon chains in the rubber of your tires. They do this by shortening the molecules, which cause a loss of elasticity in the rubber. Tire companies know all about this. They add two sacrificial protectants to the rubber.

Carbon black is added to protect against ultraviolet light. This is why tires don't come in designer colors to match your paint. This carbon black turns to a whitish/gray as it absorbs the ultraviolet light and dissipates the UV energy as heat. This is why your tires turn into that nasty looking gray as they age. They turn into this gray grungy mess in an attempt to save the rest of the tire.

To protect against ozone, tire companies add a wax-based, sacrificial protectant. As your tire rolls down the highway additional wax is forced to the surface of the tire. This is referred to as blooming. A tire that hasn't been flexed (or driven) in several months will have the wax depleted by the ozone and thus begin to degrade and suffer dry rot. That's why trailer tires go bad so much faster than car tires.

The raw silicone oil that's the main ingredient in most high-gloss rubber products may actually dissolve this wax. While you thought you were doing the right thing, you

This may be one of the best combinations. The good part is that while this may be an original wheel on the car, some very accurate reproductions are being made. The tire is obviously not original but it certainly looks nice. The true giveaway is that this tire is a radial Goodyear. That wasn't available in the late 1960s.

This is a Nitto All-Terrain tire on a very shiny rim. When you look at the cleanliness of the inner fender area it's doubtful that this truck has ever been on a fire trail. On the other hand, this combination gives the owner the aggressive look they wanted. My only concern is that this wheel could very well be a gravity cast wheel. Trucks need a stronger wheel.

You have to love the full-fendered street rods. It's not just the wheels and tires; it's also small details such as the exhaust pipes that exit through the rocker panels.

This is a very serious show car—even the brake caliper is polished. When you get to this low of a profile, you have very little ride comfort. Then again that really isn't the point here. Is it?

were really the cause of premature tire sidewall cracking. Just to make things worse, a lot of the nationally advertised rubber and vinyl products also contain formaldehyde. If you plan on embalming your tires, then you may wish to use one of these products.

The best quality tire dressings contain a strong UV protectant to bolster the efforts of the carbon black. They don't contain any raw silicone oil either. Some of the best tire dressings are One Grand Exterior Rubber and Vinyl Dressing and 3M Rubber Treatment and Tire Dressing. There is also another 3M product called Tire Restorer, which has shown a lot of promise. These are the best non-silicone, oil-based products available.

The best system to clean your tires is a citrus-based cleaner. Simply spray the tire with the cleaner to dissolve the wax residue. Then use a soft brush to scrub out any old dirt and the wax residue that gets into the cracks of your tires. It could very well take several applications of the citrus cleaner to remove the entire wax residue.

Once you've removed all traces of the old wax residue, wash the tire thoroughly with car wash. Rinse the tire completely with water to remove any traces of the citrus cleaner. Finally, apply a protective coating of your favorite rubber treatment product and you're done.

If you've been using raw, silicone-based products, this raw silicone oil has probably saturated into the tire. One Grand Exterior Rubber and Vinyl Dressing or 3M Rubber Treatment will help dissolve this silicone oil (a good thing) but they don't seem to be able to do this evenly (a bad thing). The finish on your tires may be slightly splotchy after the first couple of applications. Don't give up. The only solution is to apply several coats about a week apart. Let the good stuff work its magic. Eventually the finish will even out.

WHEEL CARE

You've just spent a huge pile of money on wheels. You might even think of them as an investment. At the very least you want to keep them looking good. Or, you've simply tried to make your old wheels look good so you don't have to spend a big pile of money on new ones.

The best advice is actually pretty easy. Just clean your wheels a lot and don't use wheel cleaners unless you absolutely have to. When it comes to car and truck detailing, I have one basic philosophy. Always begin with the least aggressive product.

A quality car wash solution will probably remove most of the dirt and brake dust from the wheel. Just use the very same stuff you use on the paint. If it didn't eat the paint off your fender then it's good for your wheels.

If car wash doesn't do the trick, then try a quality wheel cleaner. My two favorite wheel cleaners are both made in Germany, P21S and Sonax. Most of the popular brands are

Left: One of the nice things about street rods is how basic everything is. A front suspension doesn't get much easier than this. The front wheels and tires on this car won't require a new credit limit on your VISA card either. **Right:** Here's an owner who spent very little money and paid attention to doing it right. The hubcap and wheel are detailed beautifully. This car is truly a billet-free zone. It's also stunning.

Hoosier seems to have every niche market covered. This is what the company calls its Pro Street tire. It uses radial construction and the wide channels in the tread that will provide decent traction in the rain. Also, this tire is speed rated H, which means it's good to 130 miles per hour.

These are reproduction Silvertowns from BFGoodrich. This car is an example of what can be done on a reasonable budget. Not only would polished billet wheels cost a lot more, they would actually detract from the car.

highly acidic and may very well damage the finish on your wheels. The active ingredient in many wheel cleaners is hydrofluoric acid (the same stuff they use to etch glass). P21S and Sonax are pH balanced for the German wheel finishes. They may not be as aggressive as other brands, but neither will they strip the finish off your wheel.

Most wheel cleaners work best on a dry wheel. Spray the cleaner on the wheel and work it evenly into all the areas of the wheel with a soft cloth or sponge or one of the wash mitts. Try to smooth out any drips or runs so there's an even coating of cleaner over the entire wheel.

Allow the wheel cleaner some time to work (three to five minutes) and then gently scrub the wheel. Some areas of a dirty wheel may require gentle brushing with a soft brush to dislodge the dirt. If areas need additional cleaning, spray the wheel with more cleaner and gently brush.

You'll also want to periodically polish the wheels with a non-abrasive polish. Keep in mind that non-abrasive in the world of car care generally means a very fine abrasive so be

careful. I usually use a mixture of polish and aluminum cleaner for the stubborn spots.

A coat of car wax on the wheels will keep the dirt and brake dust from sticking to the wheel. I'm amazed at how many people will spend hours waxing their car and never touch the wheels. Waxing the wheels is probably more important than waxing the hood.

Painted Finish: When cleaning your painted wheels you need to avoid chemical wheel cleaners. Most of them contain caustic chemicals that damage the clear-coated finish by clouding it or in some cases actually removing it. If you wouldn't spray a cleaner on the hood of your car then you shouldn't be spraying it on your wheels.

The finish on your wheels is similar to your vehicle's paint job. Always use a mild detergent that's designed for use on automotive finishes. Use a washing mitt or a soft sponge. Never use any type of brush or abrasive pad as these will scratch and damage the finish.

Left: This is one incredible wheel, but I would hate to clean it. Even worse than just cleaning would be getting it rebuilt. Wire wheels need periodic tuning. The spokes loosen and the wheels actually get out of round. Only a few firms can service a wire wheel properly. *Right:* Notice how the exposed part of the wheels is the same color as the body. This is the way it was done at the St. Louis plant back in the mid-1950s.

Left: Wide whitewalls and wire wheels on a two-seater Thunderbird. Wire wheels look so good on certain cars that they may actually be worth all of the aggravation. *Right:* This is a VISA tire. They're really inexpensive and they're produced (or at least marketed) by Falken. Falken has been playing a huge role in the import market, especially with the VIP look.

You need to wax your wheels just as often as you wax the rest of the car. You probably should wax the exposed areas of your wheels three to four times a year. This will help keep the road grime and the brake dust from damaging the finish of your new wheels. Once the brake dust eats into your wheels you're done.

Clear-Coated Wheels

A lot of the new wheels are coated with a clear protective coating, which is essentially a non-pigmented, clear paint. Your clear-coated wheels should require only soap or a quality wheel cleaner product, water, and a soft brush. Once you've cleaned your clear-coated wheels, apply a coat of non-carnauba, non-abrasive polymer sealant-quality hand wax. The synthetic waxes will provide better resistance to brake dust and contaminants than a carnauba wax will. Remember, we're not protecting the wheels against airborne *continued on page 116*

continued on page 116

*Left: If you're going to show your car, spend a little time preparing it properly. Everyone has his or her own idea about the best tire-detailing product. About the only thing people agree on is that Armor-All may be the worst product for a serious show car. You certainly don't want all of this streaking on your car. **Right:** This is obsessive. That's a good thing if you're showing your car. Painted center caps were never a production item. Some people paint their own logos and others have them sent out. Also notice the condition of the brake caliper here. This is one very serious show tire.*

I love this car and I love Minilite wheels. The problem here is that the tire is a directional tire and it's installed on the wrong side of the car. This tire should be on the right side of the car. Please pay attention to the directional arrows on your tires. Also, this car needs longer wheel studs. The studs are at least 1/2 inch too short. The general rule of thumb is that a length of at least the diameter of the stud should be outside of the lug nut.

TORQ-THRUST WHEELS

They've been around for over 50 years now. American Torq-Thrust wheels are an icon. Today, the Torq-Thrust vintage wheel collection consists of 27 different custom wheel designs. If you go to the American Racing website, you'll notice how the brand has been extended as far as possible.

American Racing's Torq-Thrust Original Series 309 was a one-piece painted/machined alloy custom rim. In 1956 this wheel started a trend with American hot rod and muscle car enthusiasts that hasn't stopped yet. The original magnesium five-spoke American Racing Torq-Thrust, with its unique tapered curve form spoke design, is considered by many to be the most famous custom wheel of all time, and one that changed the world of racing on the strip and the street.

This five-spoke American Racing wheel was accepted on the drag strip because it seemed much lighter and stronger than stock steel wheels. This Mag wheel, as they were called in the 1960s, went from the drag strip to the streets. This one wheel actually started the custom wheel trend of the 1960s and 1970s. Sets of genuine Torq-Thrusts custom wheels are very collectible and bring some really wild prices on eBay.

This is what made America great. Huge amounts of torque from the engine, very loud pipes, and American Racing mag wheels. We surely can't go back in time but we can at least preserve it.

Left: There's a lot of discussion about what chroming does to the structure of the wheel. GM has never offered chrome wheels on a Corvette. That tells me all I need to know. On the other hand, I doubt if this car gets driven very hard at all. **Right:** This is one very rare center cap. It was only used on a commemorative edition of the Corvette that was produced to celebrate Corvette's Le Mans victory. Twenty years from now it'll be impossible to replace this center cap.

There's no longer a line between restoration and modification. This Chevy has a perfectly stock exterior with 245/40ZR/18 tires. The interesting thing with this wheel is the extreme offset. The goal was to put this much rubber under car and keep the outer edge of the tire approximately where the stock tire was.

The rear of the car continues the offset theme. Both the tire and the wheel are much wider than at the front but the outer edge of the tire is in approximately the stock location.

continued from page 113

dirt. We're talking about brake dust that can be over 500 degrees as it lands on your wheel. Carnauba just isn't tough enough to withstand that degree of heat.

Powder-Coated Wheels

Powder coatings possess significant durability and resistance to abrasion, corrosion, scratching, and chemicals when compared to liquid or solvent-based paint. Furthermore, powder coatings stay bright longer with less fading and the color selection is virtually unlimited.

The biggest problem with powder-coated wheels is that while you can touch-up nicks and chips in paint, that's something you can't really do with powder coating. While it's tougher to chip powder coating than normal paint, it can be done. One place it happens is when the tire store hammers the balance weight on your perfectly restored rim. I don't even want to think about what happens when they remove the old weight and put a new one on in a different location.

Chrome-Plated Finish

The same rules apply for chrome-plated wheels as for wheels with a painted finish. Chrome-plating is actually more delicate than paint and thus requires more care. You may wish to clean and wax them more often.

Don't use an abrasive chrome polish, as this will scratch the chrome-plating. If you live in a climate where road salts are used in the winter months you should probably remove your plated wheels during this time.

Road salt contains chemicals that break down the finish on chrome wheels. I had a set of chrome-plated Crager wheels that never made it through a second Pennsylvania winter. The chrome plating was that cheesy. Most other aftermarket companies are just as bad.

The chrome that aluminum wheels are plated with is really nice and can significantly change the appearance of your car by attracting light to base areas of your vehicle. To reflect light, which is what produces the brilliant finish, the wheels must be cleaned regularly. It's best to clean them with a soft brush, soap, and/or mild degreaser or quality spray-on wheel cleaner. Have I said this before?

Chrome will really show water spots so you might follow up with glass cleaner. Never allow soap, chemicals, or water to sit on the surface and produce water spots. As stated, it is important to keep wheels clean, not allowing road film, contaminants, and brake dust (which retains moisture) to accumulate and sit on the surface.

BRAKE PAD DUST AND YOUR WHEELS

Brake pads are made from several components, including monofilament carbon fibers, metal filings, Kevlar fibers, and polymer-based adhesives. The brake pad adhesive is the root of most of our problems. When the adhesive residue (a component of brake dust) becomes wet, it turns acidic and may etch your wheels. During braking, the metal filings become red hot and tend to "burn" tiny holes in the finish of your wheels. If you have small droplets that look like road tar on your wheels, this may not be road tar, but may in fact be re-polymerized brake pad adhesive. These polymer adhesives form droplets that wind up on the wheels where they adhere with a vengeance. The only sure way to stop all this etching/burning/flocculating is to refrain from using your brakes. Such a course of action is not usually desirable, even though some drivers are proponents. One of the keys to maintaining your wheels is a coat of wax. The wax acts as a sacrificial protectant. The damaging effects of red-hot brake dust, brake dust acids, pollution, and ozone are unleashed upon the wax and not your wheel.

Polished Aluminum

This is a major deal. Aluminum wheels look really great—when they actually shine. I own far more aluminum wheels than any sane person should. I've also tried practically every product on the market. I've concluded that almost all of the automotive products are pure junk.

There are two places to find good advice, and products, for cleaning aluminum: aircraft and Airstream trailers. Both use a lot of aluminum. Both have very fussy owners. The good part is neither group is as cheap as people in the car hobby. They demand quality products and they're willing to pay for it.

This car is beautifully detailed; the tire detailing is superb. There simply aren't too many wheels available for the C4 Corvette. The problem is that the rather extreme offset requires a very strong wheel. Cheap wheels simply won't hold up on the Corvette. The wheels have a tendency to become ovalized on the inboard edge. Rather than deal with this issue, most manufacturing companies have simply walked away from the C4. The market is small and the owners are too demanding. The Chinese marketing firms decided not to bother.

Left: This is really a show car. It may have been run on the strip once but it's really all about show. One of the constant themes of show cars is to use a racing look. At one time this was what Pro-Street was all about. What ever happened to that look anyway? Right: The competition look is carried right through to the front. This is a case where the theme is just beautifully executed. You couldn't do this without paying a lot of attention to the tires and wheels.

If you want to see how good your wheels can look just drive out to the airport and look at some of the privately owned airplanes. You're sure to find a few that will just knock you out. Or, go to an Airstream trailer show. That's even wilder. These folks take polished aluminum to a new level.

The one thing both these groups have in common is their love of a polish called Nuvite. Nuvite is even endorsed by Boeing for use on its airplanes. Once you get the aluminum to the point where you're happy, you can use lighter fluid to clean the wheels after each car wash. An alternative to lighter fluid is to use a vinegar-based glass cleaner. Just be careful not to let anything with ammonia near your wheels. Ammonia has a really nasty chemical effect on aluminum.

Left: You have to love this. It's really just a lot of bling, but it's still cool—the rubber band tires and the Wilwood brakes jump out at you. With tires like this, the ride has to be horrible but sometimes it's just about making a visual statement. Right: This is one of the dumbest ideas I've seen in a long while. The owner installed some aluminum shields between the wheel and the face of the hub. This absolutely ensures that no air will ever be able to cool the brakes. Corvette brakes can get pretty hot and blocking the flow of air over the brake caliper and brake rotor is just plain stupid.

MODULAR WHEEL INSPECTION AND MAINTENANCE

Two- and three-piece modular wheels require periodic maintenance. Most of these wheels are used on race cars so you're used to doing extra work during the off-season. You'll probably develop your own maintenance schedule, but here's an example of what you need to consider.

At the close of each racing season, disassemble, thoroughly inspect, clean, re-seal, and re-torque each wheel.

Replace wheel bolts each season.

After thoroughly cleaning all mating surfaces with an appropriate cleaner, add a thin skim coat of silicone sealant to these surfaces, assemble wheel, and torque bolts to recommended torque.

Wheel-Bolt Torque:

1/4-inch bolts need 15 lb-ft

5/16-inch bolts need 20 lb-ft

Install new valve stems.

Add a coat of silicone sealant to the drop center area of the wheel and let it cure for at least 24 hours before you mount your tires.

Nothing is quite like a full-fendered fat Buick. In a case like this you almost have to go with a reproduction tire. A modern tire just wouldn't look right. The problem is that the tires will perform as poorly as the original tires. Then again, how often do you really drive a car like this?

Left: *Everyone thought they would get rich buying the 1976 Cadillac Eldorado. This was supposed to be the last convertible. It didn't work out that way so this owner decided the hell with it and made his Caddy into a personal statement. It's not often that a spare tire gets this much attention.* ***Right:*** *This is commonly known as restofication. It's really not restored but it's close. Both the tire and the wheel are enhanced versions of what might have been installed on this Mustang several decades ago.*

CHAPTER 9
TRAILER TIRES AND WHEELS

I really hate trailers. I hate trailer ramps, tie downs, and lights. I especially hate trailer tires. The problem is that all of this stuff is essential—especially the tires. I know people who never really think about the tires on their cars. I've never really understood that, since I spend days poring over tire specifications, not to mention an inordinate amount of time at the track checking tire pressures and temperatures.

The problem is that at the end of the day I just load the car on the trailer and never give a thought to the trailer tires. I've never met anyone who actually wore out a trailer tire. They die of old age and they blow out, but they never seem to wear out.

That may very well be part of the problem with trailer tires. We just ignore them, and then bitch about them. Trailer tires are normally just abused. We put them on and never think about them until something bad happens.

The good part is the tire companies understand this. They actually make trailer tires tougher since they know no one ever really cares about them. Trailer tires are gen-erally built with tougher material and are more resistant to bruising. They're also more expensive than other tires.

Car and truck tires need to maintain traction during all driving conditions: pulling, stopping, turning, or swerving. Because of this, car and truck tires generally have more flexible sidewalls, as they need to maintain tread to road contact.

Trailers, on the other hand, have no driving torque applied to their axles. The only time trailer tires must have traction is during the application of brakes, which is pretty important when you think about it.

Trailers with heavy loads, high vertical side loads (such as camper trailers), or trailers with inadequate tongue weight can be affected by trailer sway problems. Automotive bias or radial tires with their more flexible sidewalls can actually accentuate trailer sway problems. The stiffer sidewalls of the ST (special trailer) bias-ply tires help to control and reduce sway problems. This is the reason it's not recommended that Passenger (P) or Light Truck (LT) tires be used on trailers.

*Left: Trailer tires are special. A lot of extra effort goes into making a trailer tire. All of that effort means it has a very defined purpose. You wouldn't think of putting this tire on your car. Why, then, would you consider putting a passenger car tire on your trailer? **Right:** Here's a good example how you can get in trouble if you're not careful. This trailer only has four wheels, the same number of wheels as the car inside. Each one of these trailer wheels has to support 25 percent of the weight of the car. Now add several hundred pounds of tools and several hundred more pounds of extra junk carried around because they might be needed, and there is a problem. Oh, and the weight of the trailer hasn't even been added in. You can easily see that each one of these trailer tires is being asked to carry far more than a normal passenger car tire.*

Left: When you get to the really long trailers you'll have to go to a six-wheel rig. That's because you've added not only the additional weight of the larger trailer but you have a lot more room for more heavy junk. A wheel and tire can only handle so much weight. There comes a point when you just have to put more tires under the trailer. Right: Steel wheels are very strong, and at the same time, not that expensive. The center of the wheel is a steel pressing that's welded to the rim. What they lack in elegance they more than make up for in value. The label on this wheel suggests that you torque this wheel to somewhere between 90 and 120 lb-ft. It also says that you should do this after 10 miles, 25 miles, and 50 miles, and periodically after that. Getting the idea now?

Wheels and Lug Nuts

Trailers very often have higher wheel-load capacity than passenger cars or trucks. If it's a dual-axle, enclosed trailer we just love to see how much we can cram into the trailer. If you stop and think about it for a minute you'll realize that each one of the trailer wheels is subjected to a whole lot more weight than any one of your car's wheels. That means your trailer tires have to hold a great deal more weight than your car's tires.

You also need to remember that the tandem axles on your trailer don't steer. That means that the trailer's wheels are subjected to high twisting side loads in tight, slow turns. This causes the wheel to flex which tends to loosen wheel lug nuts over time. Always check lug nut torque before each trip. A suitable torque wrench only costs about $30 and is a worthwhile investment considering the value of your trailer.

Trailer wheel lug nut torque is usually much higher than that specified for passenger car wheels. Check your particular trailer's recommended specifications. Most are in the 90–95 lb-ft range. On a new trailer, check the torque on all wheels after the first 25 to 50 miles of towing. I would personally check the lug nuts every time I get ready to head out for the car show or track. It should go without saying that you should never drive a loaded trailer with a missing lug nut or damaged lug bolt. Then again we generally just neglect our trailers. Just don't be stupid when it comes to your trailer.

Wheel lug nuts are usually tightened in a star pattern for 5-bolt and 10-bolt wheels, crossing over to opposite sides as you work around the wheel. A cross pattern is used for 4-, 6-, and 8-bolt wheels.

Torque figures: Wheel Bolts
M10 - 40 lb-ft / 54 Nm
M12 - 65 lb-ft / 88 Nm
M14 -108 lb-ft /146 Nm
Torque figures: Nuts
3/8″ UNF - 42 lb-ft / 57 Nm
7/16″ UNF - 50 lb-ft / 67 Nm
1/2″ UNF - 56 lb-ft / 76 Nm
5/8″ UNF - 85 lb-ft / 115 Nm
5/8″ UNF - 79 lb-ft / 108 Nm

How Old Are My Trailer Tires?

Trailer tires suffer from infrequent use over a relatively long life cycle. This brings into play the normal, natural aging of tires as well as ozone damage. Together, these factors may cause the rubber to crack—especially in the tire's sidewall. Part of your trailer maintenance program should be to constantly check your trailer tires for aging. Tires that are over five years old should be inspected regularly because cracking gets progressively worse as time goes on.

You can determine the tire age by looking at the Department of Transportation number. This DOT Tire Identification Number is on one side of every approved tire. It begins with the letters DOT, indicating that the tire meets all federal standards. The next two numbers

Left: These are forged aluminum wheels from Alcoa. When it comes to this type of wheel, Alcoa is the industry leader. *Right:* The tires here are Michelin 245/70R/17.5. These are tires designed for tractor-trailer rigs. Combined with the Alcoa wheels you'll have no need to worry about tire and wheel problems.

Left: This can only be described as the budget solution. A rig such as this can actually provide good service if you pay attention to maintenance. It's a heavy trailer, but it's also very strong. *Right:* Trailer wheels can look good without spending a lot of money.

or letters are the plant code where it was manufactured, and the last four numbers represent the week and year the tire was built. For example, the numbers 3106 means the 31st week of 2006.

There was an earlier dating system that was used in the last century but if your trailer tires were constructed prior to the year 2000, I would just buy some new tires.

Tire Covers

One of the best things you can do for your trailer tires is to simply cover them when your trailer is sitting idle. I've seen a variety of ways to cover the tires and I won't bore you with

specifics. Just remember that the sun will probably do more damage than all the miles you might accumulate.

DETERMINING MAXIMUM GROSS TRAILER WEIGHT

I can't discuss trailer tires without discussing one of the biggest problems. Most of us just put too damn much stuff in, or on, our trailers. The biggest problems are with the enclosed race car trailer, which we use as a portable garage.

Your trailer's springs, axles, tires, and chassis were all designed to handle a certain maximum load. This load consists of the empty trailer itself, plus the weight of everything

Left: *It's ugly but it works. Even better it was probably reasonable. These tires are rated at 1,800 pounds. With four tires, that means the combined weight of the trailer and its load can be 7,000 pounds.* **Right:** *This steel trailer might weigh as much as the Firebird. Okay, not really, but keep in mind that steel trailers are really heavy.*

you put in the trailer. This is called the gross vehicle weight rating, or GVWR. Sometimes this is referred to as gross trailer weight or GTW.

In addition, each axle has a maximum weight that it was designed to support. This is called the gross axle weight rating, or GAWR. The total of all axle loads plus the tongue weight should not exceed the GVWR.

Cargo Capacity = GTW - Empty Trailer Weight

Overloading a trailer beyond its rated capacity, even though it may be well balanced and handle fine, is a dangerous practice. Eventually something is bound to break with some dramatic and unpleasant results. Overloading also puts excess strain on your tow vehicle. You could be setting yourself up for failures at the hitch or in your capacity to safely bring everything to a stop in an emergency. Exceeding the GTW also overloads the trailer's frame, axles, bearings, wheels, and tires.

Be very careful when it comes to homemade trailers. It is amazing how many bad ideas can be incorporated into this group. Do you really want to risk lives—your own included—saving a few bucks on a trailer? How many trailers have you seen fishtailing down the roads that were manufactured by a credible company? Probably not many. If you now own an ill-handling, no-name misfit, either get it fixed by a professional or junk it.

Good cargo trailers are usually designed to maintain a proper tongue weight if they are loaded evenly. It's up to you to find out what is the maximum GTW of your trailer. Trailers made by reputable manufacturers should have a tag

or instructions that list the loading limits.

If you have a trailer built 20 years ago by a company that no longer exists, or if the tag is missing, it could be a problem. If you can't obtain actual figures from the original manufacturer you can always take it to a reputable trailer store and get an expert to give his or her best estimate of the GTW capacity.

Load your trailer well below the maximum for the first tow or while you are learning to pull a trailer. Keep track of the weights of the individual items as you load them. When in doubt, guess high.

Adjust the load so that you have around 12 to 15 percent of your estimated total weight on the hitch. You can even eyeball your rig when it's fully loaded. Attach the trailer to the tow vehicle and note how much the rear end drops. (If it looks excessive, check the tow vehicle's load capabilities again.)

Weighing the Trailer

It's not necessary to weigh your trailer every time you load it. It is, however, a very good idea to weigh it at the beginning of the season, or whenever you decide to load even more new (and heavy) stuff into it. I prefer to disconnect the trailer while it's on the scales.

You can also weigh the trailer by having just the trailer wheels on the scale. Take the number from the scales and add the weight at the tongue. You now have your GTW.

Knowing the total weight of your trailer and the tongue weight allows you to calculate the percentage of weight that should be on the hitch. When doing this for the first time it is a good idea to also check the tow vehicle weight. Make

Left: *You know you're a bucks-up racer when you even have a spare tire for your trailer. It's amazing how many folks trailer around without a spare tire.* **Right:** *This is when you're having a bad trailer day. The little guy here is thinking about a solution for dad.*

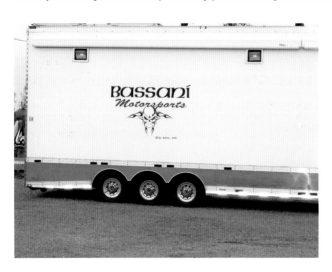

Left: *The wheels are this far back to balance out the weight of the trailer.* **Right:** *One thing you must keep in mind is that all four tires must match. At the very least the wheels and tires on a given axle must match. You might think that all tires are the same size. That's simply not the case. Each tire company varies even though the size on the sidewall might say it's the same. If you put a Goodyear on one side of your trailer then you need a Goodyear on the other side. In this case, all four tires are exactly the same model and the same brand. That's the best way.*

sure that nothing—the trailer or the vehicle—is loaded beyond the manufacturer's specifications.

SOME BASIC TRAILER TIRE GUIDELINES

ST tires feature materials and construction to meet the higher load requirements and demands of trailering.

The polyester cords in an ST tire are bigger than they would be for a comparable passenger or light truck tire.

The steel cords have a larger diameter and greater tensile strength to meet the additional load requirements.

The tire rubber compounds used in an ST tire contain more chemicals to help the tires resist weather and cracking from ozone exposure.

Inflation

Always inflate trailer tires to the maximum inflation indicated on the sidewall.

Check inflation when the tires are cool and haven't been exposed to the sun. If the tires are hot to the touch from operation, add 3 psi to the max inflation. Under-inflation is the single greatest cause of trailer tire failure.

Load Carrying Capacity

All of your trailer tires must be identical in size for the tires to properly manage the weight of the trailer.

The combined load capacity of the right and left tires should always equal (or exceed) the gross vehicle weight rating of the axle.

The combined capacity of all of the tires should exceed the loaded trailer weight by at least 20 percent. If the actual weight is not available, use the trailer GTW. Even better, load your trailer the way you would for a race weekend and then have it weighed. The results might surprise you.

If a tire fails on a tandem axle trailer, you should replace both tires on that side. The remaining tire was probably subjected to excessive loading and could have been damaged internally.

If you replace the tires on your trailer with tires of a larger diameter, the tongue height will probably need to be adjusted in order to maintain proper weight distribution.

Speed

As heat builds up, the tire's structure starts to disintegrate and weaken. A tire that has been going flat will have this problem.

The load carrying capacity of a tire gradually decreases as the heat and stresses generated by higher speed increases.

Time

Time and the elements weaken a trailer tire much more than use. After about three years of use, roughly 1/3 of the tire's strength is gone. Trailer tires should be replaced after three to four years of service, regardless of tread depth or tire appearance.

If you store your trailer outside, rig some sort of sun shield for the tires to keep the sun from drying out the sidewalls

Storage

The ideal storage is in a cool, dark garage with the tires at maximum inflation. Place thin plywood sheets between your trailer tires and the concrete floor. Put your trailer on blocks to take the weight off the tires, lower the air pressure and cover the tires to protect from direct sunlight if you leave the trailer outside.

Maintenance

Clean the tires using mild soap and water. Do not use tire-care products containing alcohol or petroleum distillates. Inspect for any cuts, snags, bulges, or punctures a few days before each trip. Check the inflation before towing and again before the return trip.

Mileage

Trailer tires are designed not to wear out. They use a very hard rubber compound compared to the average passenger car tire. The life of a trailer tire is limited by time and duty cycles. No matter the miles put on your trailer tires, you

should still install new ones every three to five years.

TRAILER TIRE WEAR

There are a number of important factors in getting the best wear from your tires. First, keep in mind that a trailer tire's tread life is directly related to the load it has to carry. Keep this in mind, and also consider it when reviewing the service you have received from your tires.

Since we're discussing car trailers here, as opposed to snowmobile trailers, you're probably subjecting your trailer to maximum loads all the time. I can't remember the last time I saw a car trailer lightly loaded. If we can find room we'll load more on the trailer.

All of this weight will rather obviously be transferred to the tires. You'll wear out your tires more from overloading than you will from normal tread wear. The bad part is that by doing this, you're breaking down the internal structure of the tire, which you can't see.

TIRE CARE DURING STORAGE

When you park your trailer for an extended time period, make sure the trailer is as level as possible. This is especially crucial if you have an enclosed trailer since they're fairly heavy. Besides, you're probably using your enclosed trailer as a garage, leaving the car, a golf cart, and whatever else in the trailer all winter

Leveling the trailer helps avoid tire overload, which can occur due to weight transfer. You can also use blocks to support the wheel positions. Take extreme care when blocking tires so that they are fully supported across the entire contact patch. Use real, curved tire blocks, not a leftover 4x4 hunk of wood with sharp edges.

You might even give some thought to using jack stands under the axles so that the tires bear no load during this period. If the trailer is left outside, cover the tires to protect them from direct sunlight and ozone aging. Keep in mind that air loss will occur over time; check and refill your tires to the correct pressures before you use it for a trip.

If you actually remove your trailer tires during the off-season you should store them in a clean, cool, dry, and well-ventilated area. Cover the tires with an opaque, waterproof material such as a plastic tarp. Treat them the same way you treat your race or show tires. Don't stack the tires so high that the bottom tire loses its shape. At the beginning of the next season, when remounting the tires, position them on the hub and tighten the lug nuts according to manufacturer's torque specifications.

SOME BASIC GUIDELINES FOR TOWING

Check Your Trailer Before Each Trip: Make sure that the

Left: A compact trailer has a lot of advantages. This car actually overhangs the rear of the trailer. That's not a concern. The concern is that the tires and wheels are strong enough to hold the car. *Right:* A single-axle trailer has a lot of advantages. A lot of the smaller road racing cars are less than 1,500 pounds. In that case, the entire car and trailer can be supported by two tires and wheels.

Left: ST stands for Special Trailer. The sizing numbers are the usual combination of metric, percentages, and inches. *Right:* Most states require that trailer tires be covered. This is for the rain spray that gets thrown off on the highway.

pin securing the ball mount to the receiver is intact, the hitch coupler is secured, and the spring bar hinges are tight with the safety clips in place (for load equalizer or weight distributing hitches). Always make sure the safety chains are properly attached and that the electrical connections are plugged in.

Practice Backing Up: It's a good idea to practice backing your trailer in a parking lot and in a vehicle that allows you to see the trailer through the rear window. Vans and trucks with caps over the bed generally have obstructed rear views that require the use of side mirrors. That's going to take a little more practice. In any case, be patient, and make steering adjustments slowly and a little at a time. You don't want to make a complete fool of yourself at the next event.

Watch Your Tongue Weight: Too much weight on the tongue will cause the rear of the trailer to sway and make the tow vehicle difficult to control. The tongue weight shouldn't exceed 200 pounds for a trailer up to 2,000 pounds. Tongue weight for trailers over 2,000 pounds should be 10 to 15 percent of the trailer's loaded weight.

Take Care of Your Tires: Check your tires for wear, cuts, or other damage and replace as needed. Most important, though, is to maintain the tire pressure recommended by the manufacturer, located on the tire sidewall. Check this before each trip.

Keep the Bearings Greased: Wheel bearings are the heart of trailers. They need to remain tight and packed with fresh grease. Poorly greased bearings will overheat and deteriorate, creating serious problems if they fail. Inspect and repack your bearings once a year. Place your hand on the wheel hubs whenever you stop on a trip. If they feel unusually warm, you may have a problem.

Watch Your Weight: When loading, balance the cargo with 60 percent of the weight near the front. Front-engine cars can be driven straight on to a trailer. Your Formula Ford should probably be backed on.

Secure the Trailer: Keep the safety chains fastened securely to the tow vehicle in case the hitch fails. Cross the chains under the trailer tongue and allow slack for turning. For additional security, padlock the trailer hitch to the tow vehicle. This will also prevent someone from stealing the trailer while you're staying at a motel.

Check the Lights: Before you begin a trip, ask someone to step behind the trailer to make sure the taillights, brake lights, and turn signals are working properly. If the lights are dim there's a bad connection. An occasional shot of WD-40 into the wiring connector reduces corrosion. Also check the ground wire on the trailer.

Go Wide on Turns: The trailer tends to cut corners more sharply than the tow vehicle. You don't want to hit things. If you keep hitting curbs you're going to cause tire damage. More important, you'll momentarily lose control of the trailer. That's not a good thing.

You don't have to spend a lot of money to have a good-looking trailer. The only change I might make in this situation is to switch over to real trailer tires. While this tire will support the trailer, the added sidewall rigidity of an ST tire might improve things on long highway tows.

THREE KEYS TO AVOIDING TRAILER TROUBLE

- Make sure your rig is equipped with the proper tires.
- Maintain the tires meticulously.
- Replace trailer tires every three to five years, whether they look like they're worn out or not.

This is why we need strong wheels on our trailers. The saving grace here is that this vintage midget is very light. On the other hand, the owner has managed to store a bunch of tires and several gas cans on this trailer. Then he's asking all of this to be supported by two passenger car wheels and tires. It's not a problem with this midget but you get the idea.

CHAPTER 10
BASIC TIRE ISSUES

Your neighbors take care of tires the easy way. They walk into a tire store and ask how much a set of tires will cost. They then hand over the VISA card to the salesperson and go have a cup of coffee. They return in an hour and drive the car home. For some reason, we can't do that. We're tire junkies.

We spend endless hours talking about tires with other tire junkies we know. We pour over all of the information at The Tire Rack website (www.thetirerack.com). Finally, we make a decision about what tire to purchase. At which point we're confronted with the very simple fact that these tires have to be mounted on some wheels. For true tire freaks, this tire-mounting experience is an anxiety-producing moment.

We all have stories about our friends. I have one friend who had the tire store grind the epoxy coating off of his Ferrari wheels so the stick-on wheel weights would stick better. Hey, at least they had stick-on balance weights and didn't try to hammer bare lead weights on the edge of the rim. You know how that whole thing was resolved. He ended up owning one screwed-up set of Ferrari wheels. Oh well.

Let's do some reflecting on some basic mounting issues. You'll still have some anxiety, but at least you can be an informed consumer.

MOUNTING YOUR TIRES

I think having new tires mounted is one of the most anxiety producing experiences when it comes to your car. One little slip and your thousand-dollar wheel is toast. Since most of us really can't mount our own tires, we have to pay someone and leave our expensive wheels at the mercy of the shop.

Over the past decades, the mounting machines have gotten better and better, and the people who operate them seem to have gotten worse. Too often the mounting of tires is handed over to the newest, and youngest, person in the shop. That's not good for you—it's even worse for your wheels.

You've probably already gone out and purchased the lowest profile tires you can find, and you now own the widest possible tire that can fit on your wheel. Life couldn't get any harder for the guys at the tire store.

Before you turn your wheels over to the tire guys, take a look around the shop. My basic rule is that if they don't give a damn about how the shop looks, they probably don't care much about your wheels either. Too many shops are what the industry refers to as a production shop. In other words, how can we maximize profit? The goal is to get as much work as possible into the shop and then get it out the door just as quickly.

Next take a look at the equipment. What will they be using to mount your tires? There are several choices here.

Left: I'm not sure what's going on with the wheel weights. Notice that there's a sizable space between the two sets of weights. I strongly suspect that the operator only got close with the first set. Then they had to add a second set to get it right. *Right:* It doesn't get much better—or more expensive—than this. This is a Ferrari race wheel. After the balance weights were stuck to the wheel, tape was applied over the weights as an insurance policy. You should also notice the valve stem is all metal and bolted in place.

BASIC TIRE ISSUES

128

Left: Torque Thrust wheels have to be the single most popular aftermarket design in the history of wheels. Here's the Ford version on a 2007 GT-H Mustang. This is in a 17-inch model. When American Racing created the original, 15-inch was all you could get. The original design didn't even allow for the use of disc brakes. This is the one wheel design that just won't go away. *Right:* Speaking of retro. A P/T Cruiser with Moon hubcaps. If the American Racing Torq Thrust wheel is a design that won't go away then this is the hubcap that won't go away. Originally designed for the dry lakebeds of southern California, it is still with us some 60 years later. One question though, where's the tire valve?

Center-Post Mounting Machines

This is the old standard machine for tire mounting. The wheel is placed over a steel post and then clamped to the machine with a center cone through the center of the wheel. The center-post tire changer was designed years ago for servicing of steel rims. I've mounted thousands of wheels with these old machines. I've never bent a wheel using a center-post machine (which may have more to do with luck than skill). They're not a bad machine, they're just an old design.

The problem is that we continue to use much larger wheels, lighter materials, and lower aspect ratio tires. All of this means that greater stress is placed at the center of the wheel during the process of breaking the tire bead from the wheel. As a result, the wheel is very susceptible to bending during the bead-breaking process. That's not a good thing. It might even be a very expensive thing.

This old equipment is really inadequate when servicing the newer tire and wheel combinations. Several technicians have to gang up and force the new tire onto the rim with pry bars. Shop remedies are created to overcome the inadequate performance of the equipment. These attempts are dangerous to both your wheel and the technicians using the equipment.

The big problem is that if a shop only has a center-post mounting machine, it means the shop is not investing in new equipment. It might also mean the shop owner is cheap and attempting to maximize profits. It could also mean that the shop doesn't do enough business to justify the investment in new equipment. These are red flags. Don't leave your wheels in this type of shop.

Rim-Clamp Mounting Machines

This is pretty self-explanatory. The wheel is held to the mounting machine by clamps on the rim. This is much better than clamping the wheel by the center.

But just having a rim-clamp machine isn't enough. A steel clamp can put some nasty scratches in your wheels. Check to see if the clamps are padded. Hunter machines come with these pads already installed, while others can be padded with duct tapes. You have every right to look at the equipment that's going to be used on your wheels. Exercise that right.

MOUNTING DIRECTIONAL TIRES

A lot of high-performance tires are designed to only roll in one direction. This is done in an effort to improve traction. If you have directional tires, make sure you point this out to the shop doing your tire mounting. They're supposed to check for this, but a little reminder never hurts. Also, check to make sure your tires are going in the right direction before you drive off. It's a lot easier to correct any problems at that point than six months later.

*Left: Alignments don't get much easier than this. Here a heim joint is used on the end of the wishbone. Changing the toe setting on this street rod is simply a matter of screwing the heim joint in, or out of, the rod. When you get it set properly, simply tighten the jam nut. **Right:** The biggest advantage of using coil-over shocks is that you can quickly adjust the ride height of the car.*

*Left: This is the ultimate in valve stems. The stem is bolted to the wheel and a metal cap is screwed over the valve. I think more people would use this type of arrangement but they're not easy to find. The best place is an old-fashioned speed shop. **Right:** The biggest problem with these bolted valve stems is that they don't conform to curves. On this wheel the valve stem hole was drilled too close to the one wall. You can see how the valve stems really rest on the different parts of the rim. Once again there are no easy answers.*

Directional Tires

Always look for the rotation arrow on the tire's sidewall. This arrow is molded into the sidewall and indicates the direction in which the tire should turn.

Asymmetrical Tires

This is a special high-performance tire where the tread on the outer edge is different from the tread on the inner edge. There are even a few cases where the rubber compound varies from inner to outer edges. All of these tires should indicate on the sidewall which side should be facing outward.

Directional and Asymmetrical Tires

These tires combine both items. You have to look for "Side Facing Outwards" and the rotation arrow to determine side of vehicle.

VALVE STEMS

The valve stem is supposed to keep air in the tire. If the valve stem doesn't seal properly, air will leak at the base of the stem, or through the valve core. Quite simply, if you have a bad valve stem you're going to have a flat tire. You can spend all you want on quality tires, but if the shop you use buys cheap valve stems you're going to have a problem.

To most of us a valve stem is a valve stem. They all look the same so the shops only see the price. But one of the most serious safety issues is the cheap low-quality valve stems that are coming in from offshore manufacturers.

A lot of these valve stems are made of inferior materials that don't stand up well to ozone, heat, and cold over time. Most tire dealers don't even realize there's a difference in the long-term reliability of some of these cheap valve stems.

Many of the imported valve stems are made of natural rubber rather than EPDM (ethylene propylene diene monomer) rubber, which is a much tougher synthetic rubber used in most quality valve stems. EPDM rubber has a much broader temperature range than natural rubber, and remains flexible in the coldest weather. It also resists ozone and chemical attack that deteriorates natural rubber. After only two years of service, natural rubber valve stems dry out, becoming hard and brittle, allowing for cracks and leaks.

The materials used in China will not pass the SAE 1205-1206 ozone requirements, which is a standard created by the Society of Automotive Engineers. No vehicle manufacturer will accept a valve stem that doesn't meet this standard. Why should you?

Ask to look at the valve stem used on the particular tire you're looking to purchase. If you don't see a manufacturer's logo or country of origin on the product you should be very suspicious of it. A no-name valve stem may look and fit okay today, but how long will it last? The life of the rubber is determined by time and temperature. Many tires last a long time—up to 6, 8, or even 10 years—and you should want your valve stem to do the same.

Most valve stem suppliers feel you should always replace the valve stem when replacing a tire. Considering that your valve stem may be five years old, that's not a bad idea. Valve stems should also be inspected anytime a tire is balanced, repaired, or dismounted. A valve stem that's cracked, damaged, or leaking must be replaced.

Before installing a new valve stem, the shop should inspect the hole in the rim for nicks, burrs, corrosion, or other roughness that could damage the new valve or prevent a leak-free seal. Most valve stems are coated at the factory to maintain their appearance and to ease installation. If a lubricant is used, don't use a petroleum-based product (rubber absorbs oil). Carefully pull the valve into the hole and make sure it is properly seated.

On some light truck applications, special high-pressure valve stems may be required (refer to the pressure rating of the tires). Most passenger car and light truck valve stems are only rated to a maximum of 65 psi, so if the vehicle has high load capacity tires it will require high-pressure rated

This is an interesting wheel since it uses some sort of rivet head which is supposed to trick you into thinking it's a three-piece rim. Actually, it's just more jewelry. More important, though, is that someone improperly mounted the tire on the wheel. Look at where the yellow mark is in relation to the valve stem.

valve stems.

Never assume the old valve stem is the correct one for the application because it may have been replaced previously. Use a replacement valve stem that correctly matches the type of wheel and vehicle application. Many alloy wheels require a clamp-in style valve stem with a threaded metal nut.

On heavy-duty trucks, make sure the valve grommet is the correct size for the hole in the wheel, and that the valve stem is properly positioned for balance and to allow easy air-pressure checks.

Finally, make sure the valve core is fully seated and does not leak air once the tire has been mounted and inflated. And always install the cap to keep out dirt and moisture.

TIRE MOUNTING AND THE YELLOW DOT

Everyone tries to create round tires and wheels. All of the companies work very hard to develop new manufacturing methods to enhance the uniformity of their products. The rounder the tire and wheel, the better your car will ride and handle. Items such as radial runout, lateral runout, force

Left: *When you get to the really wide tires and wheels, mounting often becomes a two-person job. Even the best machines can only do so much.* **Right:** *This looks like something from a Steven Spielberg movie. In reality it's nothing more than a tire-mounting machine from Hunter engineering. Notice how the arms grab the wheel from the inside, rather than clamp on the rim. Once the wheel is clamped in place, the arm at the top is used to break the bead.*

variation (which is really a manufacturing defect), and imbalance can all affect a vehicle's ride quality.

When you mount your tires on the wheels you need to position the tire on the wheel to help minimize the final combination's force variation and/or imbalance. One procedure aligns the tire's measured high point of radial force variation with the measured low point of the wheel's radial runout.

Another technique simply aligns the tire's lightest spot with the wheel's heaviest spot. The tire suppliers are required to mark the tire's high point while the wheel manufacturers mark the wheel's low point. This helps the vehicle manufacturer match mount combinations that maximize new car ride quality while reducing the amount of balancing weight.

At one point in time, the valve stem hole on standard wheels indicated the optimum place to which the tire should be match mounted. However, with the advent of styled, aluminum alloy wheels, the stem position evolved into an aesthetic issue rather than a uniformity indicator.

The only way to accurately match mount replacement tires on used, original, or new aftermarket wheels is to use a tire balancer which has the ability to measure wheel runout

and tire force variations under load before the tire and wheel are installed on the vehicle. With these road force balancing machines, a colored dot might be positioned anywhere on the wheel relative to each wheel's runout measurement.

TIRE BALANCING

Every decent tire shop has a way of balancing tires. Almost none of them, though, truly understand what it means to balance a tire. We can thank the people who make the tire balancing machines for this situation. Companies such as Bear and Hunter have spent millions of dollars developing machines that can be used by someone who hasn't got a clue about what it really means to balance a wheel and tire.

This doesn't mean *you're* going to have a problem. If the technician follows the manufacturer's directions exactly, the tire and wheel will be perfectly balanced. It's only when a problem occurs that the technician is clueless. As long as you have a good wheel, and a good tire, everything all works rather nicely.

Tire and wheel balancing isn't one of the easiest things to understand. The technical definition of balance is the uniform distribution of mass on each side of an axis of rotation, where the center of gravity is in the same location

*Above: This tire has just been balanced and the final touch is to apply the tape over the stick-on weights. This tape is like an insurance policy for keeping the stick-on balance weights attached to the wheel. **Right:** This is my favorite way to break the bead loose on a wheel. First, you don't have to lift the wheel, and second, there's no possible way to break the wheel using this machine.*

as the center of rotation. Right.

Vibration is the most noticeable effect of imbalance. The key element here is that the vibration is dependent on vehicle speed and may be felt in the steering wheel, seats, or floorboard. The vibration generally becomes apparent between 40 and 55 miles per hour and changes in magnitude with greater speeds.

Actually, the vibration from an imbalance goes away as you go faster. If the vibration is caused by a worn component in the suspension, the vibration will get worse the faster you drive. If the vibration goes away as you increase the speed of your car, you have a tire balance issue, or, in fact, an imbalance issue.

There are really only two ways of balancing the tire and wheel assembly.

Static Balance: This type of balancing is achieved with the old-fashioned bubble balancer. This type of balancing machine was used for decades but the problem is that the machine does not correct for dynamic imbalance. All of the new balancing machines can be programmed to perform a static balance, which is why you seldom see the old bubble balancers around any more.

Dynamic Balance: This is performed with the common spin balancer found in shops all over the world. Here the tire is actually spun in the balancing process. With these dynamic spin balancers the tire/wheel assembly is balanced both statically and dynamically. There are hundreds of small variations in the different balancing machines but the basic principles remain the same.

TIRE BALANCING EQUIPMENT

Most shops have a tire-balancing machine that's designed to service tire/wheel assemblies that are stock equipment on mass-produced domestic passenger and light truck vehicles. This is where these shops get the bulk of their revenue. Some people have tires that are nice and easy to balance. You may need more specialized equipment. This is especially the case when you get to the 19- and 22-inch wheels.

Once you get to above-standard sized wheels, the shop will need special equipment. Tire balancing machines can get expensive. The more complex machines are very expensive. If you have some huge tires and wheels that need balancing, then you can expect to pay extra for balancing.

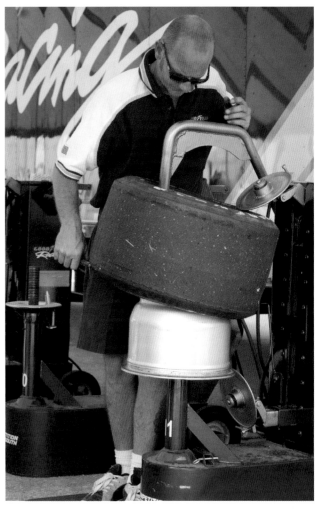

Above: *Balancing takes a little more skill than most people realize. The average tire and wheel is no problem. The problems occur when the machine calls for a huge amount of weight. The installer has to decide what is normal and when there is a problem.* **Right:** *Every tire company seems to have a favorite mounting machine. Goodyear loves this type of machine. Notice that the machine never actually makes contact with the wheel.*

All of that bling-bling isn't going to be cheap.

How Accurate Is Accurate?

The industry standard for minimum accuracy is 0.25 ounces residual imbalance when a satisfactory balance has been indicated on the machine. In other words, when the machine says your tire is perfectly balanced it may actually be 0.25 ounces out of balance. That's fine.

The balancing machine should also possess the industry standard for minimum angular position accuracy of plus or minus 5 degrees with a one (1.00) ounce static weight imbalance. In other words, the location for placing the weights may be at least five degrees from a perfect indication. Once again, that's no big deal.

Fast Is Not Necessary

A common misconception is that the tire balancer has to spin the tire at a high speed to perform a proper balance. You've probably seen the ads that promise a high-speed balance. A tire and wheel are either balanced or they're not.

Speed has nothing to do with balance. Some of these advertising guys need to go back to high school physics.

The old-style balancers required that the tire rotated at least 500 rpm, which is about 55 to 60 miles an hour. They needed this speed to pick up a usable signal. The more sensitive electronics in the newer machines can pick up a signal as low as 100 rpm, which is the same as about 10 to 15 miles per hour.

Wheel Weights

I get a little goofy about wheel weights. You have to understand that there are dozens of different wheel weights out there. People spent a lot of time designing a good wheel weight for your car. When you get new tires, the tire store just goes to the shelf and pulls down whatever weights they might have.

Shops should always use coated weights on aluminum wheels/rims to prevent damage to the finish. They also need to make sure that they're using the correct style of attachment. You have every right to ask to see the weights they intend to use on your wheels.

This means the tire is 21 inches in diameter, the tread is 8 inches, and the bead diameter is 13 inches. All of these dimensions are taken from an inflated tire without a load.

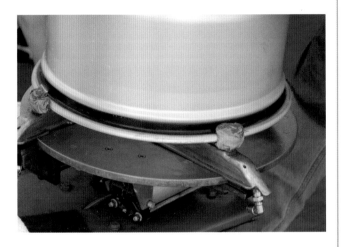

You don't want a mounting machine that eats wheels. Here Michelin has used duct tape to keep their mounting machine from digging into the wheel.

BALANCING PROBLEMS

To properly diagnose vibration problems you have to understand the types and causes of imbalance. There are really four types of balancing issues.

Static Imbalance: This is a vertical movement resulting from heavy or light spots in a tire. It can be corrected using either a static bubble balancer or dynamic spin balancer.

Dynamic Imbalance: This is a lateral movement (wobble or shimmy) resulting from unequal weight on both sides of the tire and wheel/rim assembly's circumferential centerline. This type of imbalance can only be corrected using a dynamic spin balancer.

Runout Imbalance: Runout is caused by excessive radial and/or lateral movement caused by tire or wheel/rim non-uniformity, improper bead seating, or improper match mounting of the tire and wheel/rim assembly. This can be corrected by measuring the amount of tire and wheel/rim assembly runout (both lateral and radial) with a dial gauge, and replacing the offending wheel or tire that has excessive runout.

Vehicle Imbalance: This type of vibration is due to faulty components other than the tire or wheel/rim assembly, such as hubs, brake rotors and drums, and drivelines. Correction requires checking for any irregularities, and replacement as required.

The Most Common Sources of Imbalance

The two most common sources of imbalance that occur in the tires are:
• Heavy or light spots in the tire created in manufacturing.
• Radial or lateral runout on the tire itself.
It's also very possible that balance problems can be caused by:
• Variations within the wheel, such as thickness variations and welds.
• Rotor and axle imbalances.

Step-by-Step Vibration Diagnosis

1. Inspect your tires, wheels/rims, and vehicle for irregular tread wear, damaged wheels/rims, or any vehicle component damage. Replace or adjust any worn or damaged items as might be required. Check where the wheel mounts to the hub. Make sure this area is clean and free of rust. Always tighten the lug nuts to the vehicle manufacturer's torque specification.

2. Check to be certain that the tires are inflated according to the vehicle manufacturer's recommendations and that the vehicle's suspension is working correctly. Look at the vehicle from a distance and make sure it's not tilting.

3. Check for proper tire mounting on the wheel/rim. The tire fitting line should be concentric with the rim flange.

4. Test drive the vehicle on a smooth road surface after a 5- to 10-mile warm-up to remove any flat spotting. Then try to identify exactly what is vibrating. Steering wheel vibration diagnosis should begin with front axle, wheel, and tire conditions. Floor or seat vibration diagnosis should begin with rear axle, wheel, and tire conditions. Power train and brake problems can be diagnosed by alternate brake application and transmission being placed in neutral during vibration.

5. Check the tire and wheel/rim assembly once again on the balancing machine and adjust the balance if it's required. If

Left: Before Michelin mounts a tire they carefully inspect and clean each wheel. I wish the local tire store did the same. On the other hand, I don't spend $60,000 on tires every other weekend all summer long. Right: This was a new one to me. I'm now doing it to my wheels. A very sharp putty knife removes the old stick-on balance weight about as nicely as anything I've ever seen.

the shop is unable to balance the tire and wheel, ask them to completely deflate the tire, unseat tire beads, and rotate the tire 180 degrees on the wheel. Then have them rebalance tire and wheel assembly. After that, test drive the vehicle again.

6. If the vibration is still not eliminated, measure the tire and wheel/rim assembly with a dial gauge looking for excessive lateral or radial runout. You may very well have to replace the wheel.

7. Repeat the balancing of the tire and wheel/rim assembly and once again test drive the vehicle. Some tire balance

HOW OLD ARE MY TIRES?

It's easy to identify when a tire was manufactured by reading its tire identification code (serial number). These codes identify which week and year the tire was produced.

The U.S. Department of Transportation (DOT) National Highway Traffic Safety Administration (NHTSA) requires that the code be a combination of 11 or 12 letters and numbers which identify the manufacturing location, tire size, manufacturer's code, and week and year the tire was manufactured.

The week and year the tire was manufactured is contained in the *last four digits* of the serial number. The *two digits* used to identify the week a tire was manufactured immediately precede the *two digits* that are used to identify the year.

equipment now allows steps 5 and 6 to be performed at the same time.

TIRE AND WHEEL PACKAGES

Some companies have gotten creative regarding all of these mounting problems. Companies such as Complete Custom Wheel, in Daytona Beach, Florida, will sell you a set of wheels with the tires of your choice already mounted on them. The best part is they practically give the tires away just to solve all the mounting and balancing problems.

When you take a set of custom wheels, and some wide, low profile tires to the neighborhood tire store, employees are quick to blame any problem on the parts you delivered on their doorstep. If they have a problem, they claim you brought them a bad wheel. In other words, "Not my fault." CCW solves that problem for you. When you purchase a complete tire and wheel package you simply get out your trusty jack and bolt the new rims on your car.

Other companies such as The Tire Rack (www.thetirerack.com) have created a dealer network around the country that they have confidence in. This means that if you have a problem with your tire(s), then you can simply return the tire with no questions. That also solves a lot of the traditional mounting and balancing problems. It also eliminates a lot of the traditional finger pointing that we've all experienced over the years.

USING NITROGEN FOR INFLATION

Nitrogen is the next great thing for your tires. Maybe. We're constantly being told that if we fill our tires with pure nitrogen we'll get better gas mileage, our tires will be safer, and they'll even last longer. You can't do much better than that.

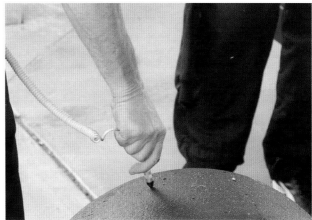

Left: At this point we're way past any tire pressure gauge I've ever owned. First, it costs $300. Next, it gives you a digital readout in tenths of a pound. It also comes with a really nice case. Oh yeah. *Right:* If you liked the Intercomp tire pressure gauge you'll love the digital pyrometer with a memory. Oh, and besides checking the temperature of your tires it will also act as a timer. It can time four cars for 100 laps in the memory. All that for $400.

Hell, it may even be true. Is it worth the cost though?

Nitrogen is a colorless, odorless, tasteless gas that makes up about 78 percent of Earth's atmosphere. Nitrogen helps keep tires cooler under highway conditions, and it's less likely to leak out, so that should help with fuel mileage. The problem is that it's going to cost anywhere from $2 to $10 per tire to fill. How much do you drive?

Nitrogen isn't cheap for the tire dealers either. The nitrogen generator and associated equipment typically run between $3,000 and $15,000. Then that shop is going to recover that investment the only way they can—by charging you.

Another problem is that tires can leak air in a variety of ways such as the tire/rim interface, valve, the valve/rim interface, and even the wheel itself. Nitrogen is of no use in these situations.

The main arguments *for* nitrogen include three points:

1. Nitrogen molecules are larger than oxygen molecules, so they migrate through the tire three to four times slower. The result: Tires hold their pressure longer.

2. Nitrogen runs about 20 percent cooler. Less heat results in less tire degradation.

3. Nitrogen drastically reduces oxidation on the rim and inner-liner (nitrogen systems almost totally eliminate oxygen—the cause of oxidation—from the mix). In other words the insides of your wheels won't rust or corrode.

Now, though, what happens if your tire pressure drops and you're not near a garage or tire store that sells nitrogen? You can fill the tire with compressed air and it won't hurt a thing. The real problem is that the tire will have to be purged and refilled with nitrogen later. More money.

Tire companies are taking a skeptical approach to nitrogen. Goodyear sees no problem with using nitrogen but is skeptical about the cost savings. Michelin officials recommend nitrogen only for tires used "in a high risk environment and/or when the user wants to reduce the consequences of a potential abnormal overheating of the tire-wheel assembly (for example in some aircraft applications)," according to a company statement. But when it comes to all other tires in normal use, nitrogen is not required and does not necessarily bring the expected benefit.

A lot of people like using nitrogen because that's what race teams use. Let's think about why race teams use nitrogen. Nitrogen is simply more consistent than normal air because air typically contains varying amounts of moisture due to changes in the relative humidity on race day. Water causes air to be inconsistent in its rate of expansion and contraction. So, a humid race in the southeast United States or a dry race in the desert western United States could make for unpredictable tire pressures if "dry" nitrogen were not used.

This brings us full circle in the nitrogen discussion. It's all a matter of cost. The only downside is the cost of inflation. That has to be a personal decision.

TIRE PRESSURE GAUGES

I've probably purchased more tire gauges than any 10 people in my neighborhood. I have one drawer in my tool chest that is testimony to my obsession with tire pressure gauges. I even have different gauges for different purposes. That's probably a problem that can only be cured with medica-

Left: Stick-on wheel weights are wonderful. The biggest problem is the mess they leave when you try to remove them. I've found that brake-cleaning solvent works nicely. Right: The clip-on balance weights work nicely and don't mar the finish on your wheel.

tion. Or, by purchasing even more tire gauges.

The advantage of having all of these tire gauges is that it's easy to check on the accuracy of any one gauge. I pick a tire and then use three or four of my gauges on that tire. They should all read within a pound of each other. If one gauge is several pounds off from the other two, I just throw it away. All I'm doing is calibrating the gauges against each other.

Digital tire gauges are kind of nice but they don't seem to hold up as well as the mechanical gauges. The old style pencil gauge is still the industry standard. It seems that the digital gauge is what you get for Christmas when the family runs out of ideas.

TIRE PRESSURE MONITORING SYSTEMS

This seems really simple to me. Your car either came equipped with an electronic tire pressure monitoring system (TPMS) or it didn't. I don't know of a single person who has installed an aftermarket system. (So much for that idea.) Actually, some of the aftermarket systems are not a bad idea. The problem is you have to spend at least $500 by the time you're done. Hell, you can get a bigger amp for the stereo system for that sort of money.

TPM systems generally use radio frequency technology to avoid expensive and rather complicated wiring. An electronic control unit is placed inside the vehicle, which provides the necessary processing power to interpret pressure data coming from the sensors and delivers alerts and warnings to the driver. Companies such as Schrader have designed a system made of radio transmitter sensors mounted on a standard tire valve and a dedicated radio fre-

quency receiver.

There are basically two types of tire pressure monitoring systems (TPMS).

Direct: The direct TPMS delivers real-time tire pressure information to the driver of the vehicle, either via a display or a simple low-pressure warning light. These systems employ actual pressure sensors inside each tire and send that information from inside the tire to your dashboard.

Indirect: An indirect TPMS measures the air pressure indirectly by monitoring individual wheel speeds and other signals available in the vehicle. Most indirect TPMS use the fact that an under-inflated tire has a slightly smaller diameter than a correctly inflated tire and therefore has to rotate more times to cover a specific distance to detect under-inflation. These systems can detect under-inflation in up to three tires simultaneously but not in all four since the operating principle of these systems is to compare the different wheel speeds. If all four tires lose the same amount of air there's no comparison and the relative change will be zero.

Some of the latest developments of indirect TPMS can detect simultaneous under-inflation in all four tires thanks to a vibration analysis of individual wheels or analysis of load shift effects during acceleration and/or cornering.

Indirect TPMS is cheap and easy to implement since most modern vehicles already have wheel speed sensors for anti-lock braking systems and electronic stability control systems. The disadvantage is that they rely on the user resetting the system when the tires are changed or re-inflated. Forgetting to perform this initialization leads to potentially dangerous false or missing alerts.

TIRE-INFLATION MAINTENANCE TIPS

Don't judge the tire pressure by eyeballing a tire. Modern radial tires bulge slightly, making them look a little under-inflated, even when they're not.

Use a tire gauge to check the pressure in all four tires and the spare at least once a month. A tire-pressure gauge is available for as little as $3 to $5 at auto parts stores. Break down and buy one.

Set the tires to the automaker's recommended tire pressure. This is printed on a placard in the car, either on a doorjamb, the fuel-fill door, or on the inside of the glove-compartment lid. Don't go by the "maximum inflation pressure" imprinted on the tire. If your car has a limited-service spare, also check that it's inflated to the pressure specified on the placard—usually 60 psi.

Measure the pressure with the tires cold, before they've been driven more than a mile or two. As the vehicle is driven, the tires heat up and the pressure rises, which makes it more difficult to set them to the correct cold-tire pressure.

This one usually baffles a lot of people. This is a center lock wheel and what you're looking at is a tie-down. The red object threads onto the axle and provides a really handy way to tie the car down inside the trailer.

TIRE REPAIR

A lot of tire repair shops will only repair a tire by placing a patch on the inside of the tire. This involves removing the tire from the wheel, remounting it once the tire has been repaired, and rebalancing the assembly. This is not going to be cheap.

There are three things you need to consider when you have a punctured tire. First, you need to evaluate the damage the object caused as it punctured the tire. The goal is to establish an airtight seal of the tire's inner liner, and completely fill the path the object took through the tire. Typically a mushroom-shaped patch and plug combination repair is considered to be the best method of repairing a punctured steel-belted radial.

Any puncture or injury to a tire's tread area obviously affects performance and safety. Proper repair is critical. The puncture must be repaired on both the inside and the outside of the tire. Because all parts of a tire are engineered to function as a single unit, any repair must take that into consideration. Only small, straight-through ¾₆-inch diameter or less punctures in the tread area may be repairable, if no secondary damage has occurred. There is a limit as to what can actually be repaired.

Generally a tire repair can be properly done only if the tire is removed from the rim. The best repair is made from the inside out. Any repair must fill and seal the injury, e.g., a vulcanized plug and patch. Keep in mind that any tire repair will void the speed rating of that particular tire. That's one good reason to consider just buying a new tire.

TIRE AGING

Tires used to wear out. Some still do. Some tires, though, seem to last forever, or at least too long. The old bias-ply tires wore out in about 15,000 miles during two years of service. By the 1980s, radial-ply tires lasted about 40,000 miles during four years of service. You can now find tires that last 60,000 to 80,000 miles

How long will tires last before aging out? The U.S. National Highway Traffic Safety Administration and tire manufacturers are currently studying the many variables. Tire life ultimately depends on the tires' service conditions and the environment in which they operate. The really difficult task remains how to confirm and quantify all of this. Of course the government thinks we need a bunch of new rules and regulations—not that it should surprise you.

The British started this whole mess. Really. The British Rubber Manufacturers Association (BRMA) says that "BRMA members strongly recommend that unused tires should not be put into service if they are over six years old and that all tires should be replaced 10 years from the date of their manufacture."

Then in 2005, the Japanese joined in. The Japan Automobile Tire Manufacturers Association (JATMA) issued a bulletin stating that "customers are encouraged to have

All balancing machines operate the same way and all seem to do a good job. Keep in mind that finding the imbalance in the tire/wheel assembly doesn't require a great deal of speed. It requires sensitivity. The new machines can do a really nice job at a really slow speed.

Always ask to see the weights the shop intends to use on your wheels. I'm sure that you have a preference about the type of weight. This is the basic clip-on weight so loved by tire shops. It's cheap, effective, and easy to install.

The new machines are really user friendly. Even better is that each new generation of machines is increasingly more precise.

their vehicle tires promptly inspected after five years of use to determine if the tires can continue to be used" (they recommend that spare tires be inspected as well). Furthermore, even when the tires look usable, it is recommended that all tires (including spare tires) that were made more than 10 years ago be replaced with new tires. In some cases automobile makers stipulate in the owner's manual the timing of tire inspections and replacement.

It was then inevitable that European car manufacturers would jump on the bandwagon. Makers of some high performance sports cars, coupes, and sedans state in the owner's manuals of these cars, "under no circumstances

RADIAL FORCE VARIATION

In the tire manufacturing process, the tread is applied as a slab of uncured rubber compound. If the tread joint is too big, then there's a heavy spot on the tire, which leads to balance problems. This balance problem is normally overcome by applying the small lead weights to the rim of the wheel. With radial tires there are tire vibrations that can't be corrected by balancing. This is because the radial tire has a flexible carcass and a very rigid steel belt. This leads to variations in stiffness around the tire, which show up as "out of round" when the tire is inflated.

To identify this problem, tire companies introduced a quality check at the end of the production process. The tire was inflated on a pair of metal flanges to represent the wheel and then rotated, measuring the variations in diameter, by means of a clock gauge. This measurement was called radial runout, and the machine was referred to as a uniformity machine.

That's why "tire uniformity," rather than "balance," has become the term used within the industry when discussing tire vibrations. The vehicle manufacturers worked to develop a machine for measuring this type of vibration, which became known as a uniformity machine. They were introduced into the tire factories as a quality check at the end of the production process.

The first uniformity machine consisted of a large-diameter metal wheel to represent the road surface and a pair of flanges to inflate the tire and present it to the wheel under load. As the tire/wheel assembly rotated, sensitive electronic equipment measured the variations in forces transmitted to the wheel by the tire.

Radial force variation (RFV) measures the uniformity of a tire. It is measured on a road-force variation machine and the results are expressed in g/cm (grams per centimeter) in Europe or inch/ounces in the United States. The vehicle manufacturers set the selection limits. Tires outside limits were diverted into less sensitive markets, or eventually scrapped. These machines are now common in tire shops. The road-force balancing machines are very expensive, so you'll probably pay a premium. It's worth it, though.

should tires older than six years be used" on the vehicle.

While American driving conditions don't include the high-speed challenges of the German Autobahn, Chrysler and Ford Motor Company joined their European colleagues in 2005 by recommending the tires installed as original equipment be replaced after six years of service. So far General Motors has declined to offer a recommendation until a more scientific analysis of driving conditions and tire aging is completed.

The real problem is that the tire you buy may already be several years old. Even worse, when a tire company clears out a warehouse this clearance sale usually includes new tires that are several years old.

Most street tires have a useful life of between 6 and 10 years. Part of that time, however, is spent as the tire travels from the manufacturing plant to your car. Thus, the best way to determine a tire's age is to count the time it's actually on your car or truck. That is roughly about six years.

Cross-section view of a tire mounted on a rim.

Tire Dimensions and Terminology

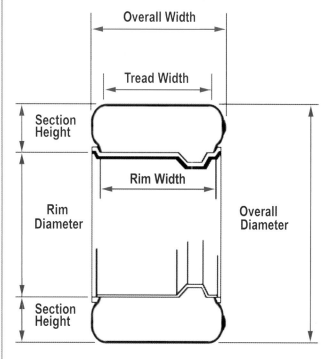

CHAPTER 11
TIRES AND ALIGNMENT

An alignment is nothing more than setting the wheels on your car in such a way that your car drives straight down the road. It means that all four wheels are pointing in the same direction and making contact with the road in an appropriate manner. Sure there are a lot of nuances, but it all comes back to how the car drives.

There are really two tests to check if your car needs an alignment. First, as was mentioned, does the car drive down the road in a straight line? Next, are your tires wearing evenly? Sometimes we just make this stuff too hard. These two tests apply to all cars, and all types of roads. It makes little difference whether you're driving down the back straight at Sebring, or going down a side street near your home.

Tires won't correct an alignment problem, but an alignment problem can correct a tire problem. In other words a bad alignment will quickly wear out your tires. It can also make your car very unpleasant to drive. I know because I have a Porsche 911 in my garage that wants to go to the left as I drive down the road.

If your car isn't properly aligned, your tires won't work properly. They'll generally wear out much faster than you had planned. In fact, they'll probably wear out on one edge leaving the other edge of the tire with a bunch of tread. A wheel alignment consists of adjusting the angles of the wheels so that they are perpendicular to the ground and parallel to each other. The purpose of all these adjustments is to ensure maximum tire life and a vehicle that tracks straight and true when driving along a straight and level road.

You really don't need an alignment as often as you might think. The only real reason to get an alignment is if something has changed since the last time you had an alignment. Hitting a huge pothole could be one such thing. After you bounce out of the pothole with a bent wheel, you're probably going to need an alignment.

Another reason for an alignment is that all of the cumulative wear in your steering and suspension system has finally caught up with you. This one is a little tricky since this wear takes place gradually. Wear is something you adjust to. Often, it's not until someone else drives your car that the poor alignment is called to your attention.

In my case, I have a third reason. I like to mess with

This is a lot of negative camber, and yes it works just fine. Race teams are really pushing the limits on negative camber. In a lot of cases they're going way beyond what the tire companies perceive as safe. The cars are incredibly fast, but the life expectancy of the tire is drastically reduced.

the car and add different parts. I'm pretty good with alignment settings, but eventually I get so far out of the ballpark that I have to put the car on an alignment rack and get everything back to some sort of baseline.

The best way to keep track of your car's alignment is to check on the tread depth of all four tires. Remember, your tires should wear evenly across the entire width of the tread. If they aren't doing this then you probably have an alignment problem

Anytime you begin to notice excessive edge wear you have an alignment problem. If the center of the tire is wearing quicker than the outside edges you've been putting too much air in your tires. On the same note, if both edges are worn the same but there is a lot of tread in the middle then you haven't been keeping enough air in the tires. If you keep track of all this on a semi-annual basis you'll probably save a little money on tires.

The best way to tell what the suspension is doing is to measure the temperature of the tire as it comes off of the car. Here the Kumho engineers check the tread temperatures. This will be done at three points across the tread. The idea is for the temperatures to be even all across the tread. Understanding what the temperatures mean takes training and experience.

Some people feel that an annual alignment is worth doing. That's only the case if you've found a good alignment shop. If you end up in a bad shop you're going to end up paying for a lot of parts and work you really didn't need.

WHERE TO GO FOR AN ALIGNMENT

Finding someone to align your car is a major ordeal. Few people are left in the service industry who can align a car properly. I used to train service technicians and only about 10 percent of the people who claim to be an alignment specialist have any real grasp of what's going on. It takes a certain amount of intelligence and experience to be an alignment specialist. Most shops can neither attract, nor retain, this type of person.

Also, keep in mind that the alignment equipment is a huge profit center for most shops. Too often the only reason the shop purchased an alignment rack was to sell a lot of suspension parts. Many of which may not actually be needed.

There are three reasons you might get a larger bill than you planned on. First, your car is actually worn out and needed these parts. Yes, that's actually the case sometimes. A second reason for the big bill is that the technician has no real idea about how to check suspension parts for wear. They may have no training or the training they received was just totally wrong.

A third reason is that the shop, or the technician, is involved in fraudulent behavior. Most technicians are paid on some sort of a commission basis. The more work they can talk a customer into the more money they make. It's probably not the best system, but it's the system we have in this industry.

It's almost impossible to pay for a modern alignment rack simply doing alignments. The alignment equipment is outrageously expensive and competition holds down the amount of money that a shop can charge for a four-wheel alignment. This means a shop has to do more than just align your car. They have to find parts to replace. In a perfect world you would actually need those parts. Given the amount of incompetence and fraud in the service industry that's too seldom the case.

You have two basic rights at this point. You have a right to see how the technician discovered the defective parts. They have an obligation to demonstrate to you why the part is defective, and what problems this worn-out part will cause.

The second right is you are entitled to have the old parts returned to you. Having the old parts returned to you means that they actually have to replace the part in question. Yes, Virginia, sometimes people pay for parts that don't actually get placed on the car. Asking for the old parts back is one way to make sure you're getting the part replaced that was in question.

All of the major car manufacturers ask dealerships to retain parts that are replaced under warranty. They then have the right to actually inspect those parts. It's interesting that they do this on a regular basis but very few consumers exercise the same right. Remember, those are your parts. You have a right to them. Just asking for the old parts puts the shop on alert. That's not a bad thing.

Even if you don't get hit with a fraudulent parts diagnosis you may not actually get a real alignment. Chances are that when you go to pick up your car you'll be handed a before and after computer printout. That is absolutely meaningless. Trust me, I can get the alignment machine to read out anything I want.

The best way to tell if a car is at the correct height is to weigh the car on all four corners. While most race teams have a set of scales to perform this procedure, the average shop has never seen one. If you find a shop that can set your car's ride height make sure you find out how much they charge. It's not going to be cheap.

In the industry it's called a "toe and go." Most of the time the toe setting is the real problem. Camber and caster are much less of a problem. One way to make serious money on an alignment machine is to simply set the toe on the car but charge for a four-wheel alignment.

There's a way to avoid this ripoff. Before you take your car into the alignment shop, paint little white (or yellow) stripes on all of the nuts and bolts that have to do with alignment. When you pick up your car you can quickly identify if anything has actually been moved. It's impossible to do an alignment without moving the nuts and bolts.

After all of this ranting you might very well wonder how to pick a good alignment shop. The best way is to look at the condition of the equipment. It doesn't have to be new, but it should be clean. Look to see how the alignment heads are put away after each alignment. Are there parts and grit from last week's application of oil dry on the floor?

Alignment equipment is very fussy. It needs to be treated properly. A bad technician will abuse the equipment, and the shop owner who has to pay the bill will simply let the equipment go to hell. You want to avoid a shop where this is taking place.

The newest alignment equipment is designed to do two things. First, the equipment has to be very easy to use. Because of the commission form of compensation, a technician will make more money if he can do more alignments each day. The time it takes to set the car on the lift and mount the alignment heads on your wheels has a direct impact on his paycheck.

The latest equipment won't necessarily mean you get a better alignment. It simply means that it will let the technician do it faster. At the end of the day the technician and shop owner should take home more money. There's noth-ing wrong with that—as long as your car gets aligned properly.

A second point to consider is that the latest equipment is designed to make up for the lack of skill that most alignment technicians bring to the job. The problem is that no amount of expensive equipment is going to make up for a tech who doesn't know the difference between caster and camber.

THREE IMPORTANT MEASUREMENTS

There are three important measurements when a car is aligned. They are: toe, caster, and camber.

We'll get to some more arcane terms a little later in the chapter, but for now we'll just stick with these three.

Toe: The first word you're going to hear is "toe." Toe is how straight the wheels are when you drive down the road. Think about this for a minute. You want the right front wheel going down the road parallel to the left front wheel. And then both of them should be parallel to the center of the car. In an ideal world, all four wheels should be parallel to the center of your car as you drive down the road.

If the wheels are cocked in toward the center of the car, we say that the wheel has toe in. If the wheel is pointing to the outside of the car we call it toe out. Anytime your car's wheels point too far from the centerline of the car you have a problem. In fact, most abnormal tire wear comes from improper toe settings.

There are times when you may want the wheels to toe-out, and we'll get to that shortly. Toe numbers are usually given in degrees. There are cases though where the number is given in inches, but that's the older system that was used before the computer age.

Toe numbers are given in inches in racing. That's because

One of the tricks when weighing the car is to make sure the weight of the driver is factored into the total weight. Since it's hard to make a driver sit still for more than five seconds, teams carry weights that are placed into the driver's seat during the weighing process. More cynical crew members will point out that this is the smartest occupant of the seat all weekend.

Left: Most race teams use this system for alignment. Here the mechanic is setting a bar in place that is exactly 90 degrees to the centerline of the car. **Right:** A similar bar is placed at the rear. Once again, this bar is exactly 90 degrees to the centerline of the car. This also means that it is perfectly parallel to the bar at the front.

most teams use the string alignment system shown in the pictures here. The string system is dead accurate when done properly, and it can be done anyplace. The new laser systems will probably replace the traditional string, but not yet.

The laser system is really just a variation of the old-fashioned string system. Instead of nylon string, a laser beam is shot down the side of the car. Think of it as being high-tech string.

Don't forget that the rear toe specifications are every bit as important as the front toe settings. Just as you don't want the front tires going down the road pigeon-toed, you don't want the rear tires doing that either.

In the past, most vehicles would have front toe-in. This gave good vehicle stability, and as vehicle speed increased, the tire resistance would cause the toe to change to the straight-ahead position. Now, some front-wheel-drive cars use offset wheels (the bolt flange is not positioned in the center of the width of the wheel), which requires that static toe settings to be out.

As the car drives down the road, the loads placed on the tires cause the wheels to turn in to the straight-ahead position. Whether the specifications call for toe-in or toe-out, they should be followed closely.

Toe-out on a rear axle can cause unpleasant spins during braking or on corners, especially on wet or icy roads. Again, solid rear axles (such as an older Mustang or Camaro) should have a 0 toe reading; anything other than 0 means that the axle is bent or out of position in the vehicle.

Incorrect toe settings can wear tires quickly. I've seen a new tire worn out in only a few thousand miles because the toe setting was out dramatically. Even if it is out a little, tire life is shortened considerably.

The most common solution is adjusting the rear toe to

*Left: Both the front and rear tubes have groves milled into them that allow for the attachment of nylon string. With the addition of the nylon string we've essentially created a box around the car. **Right:** The string is adjusted so that it's absolutely equal distances from the wheel hub. The hubs serve as a reference point.*

the centerline and then adjusting the front toe to match the rear. This is normally done during a four-wheel alignment, as long as the rear toe is adjustable.

It's important to remember that rear toe is just as important as front toe, especially on cars and minivans with front-wheel drive or vehicles with independent rear suspensions. If rear toe is off the mark, it can create a rear axle steer condition that a simple front wheel alignment check will never detect or cure.

Rear toe is also different from front toe in that front toe

REAR-WHEEL DRIVE WITH REAR LEAF SPRINGS

This is the setup of your basic pickup truck, and almost all of the cars built before 1970. This might be the most common type of vehicle on the road today. It's very low tech and it's very easy to align—unless something is wrong.

It may seem silly to pay for a four-wheel alignment on this type of vehicle, but it could help you diagnose a big problem. If the rear axle on this type of vehicle has a thrust angle, something is seriously wrong. A thrust angle here means that the rear axle has shifted, or perhaps the mounting points for the spring have moved. This is an indication that this vehicle may have been in an accident.

The next step is to look at the setback of the front wheels. Setback is a diagnostic angle that measures the difference between the centers of the front wheels. If one wheel is behind, or in front, of the other one, you have a real problem. It could be as simple as a set of junk control arm bushings, or it could be as bad as a poorly designed frame.

misalignment tends to be self-centering. When the front wheels are toed-in or toed-out with respect to one another, the two wheels share the toe angle equally while rolling down the road with tread wear being about the same for both tires. With rear toe that's not necessarily true because the rear wheels are not free to steer nor are they tied together with a steering linkage.

On a rear-wheel-drive car or truck with a solid rear axle, a cocked axle will toe-in one wheel and toe-out the other by an equal amount. This kind of misalignment will make the vehicle dog track and create a thrust angle that induces a steering pull as well as toe wear in the front wheels (turning the wheels, even slightly, causes them to toe-out which can increase tread wear).

If the rear axle misalignment can't be corrected by repositioning the spring mounts, installing aftermarket offset control arm bushings, or trying other measures, you can at least minimize the problem by aligning the front wheels to the rear thrust angle.

On applications that have an independent rear suspension, or front-wheel-drive minivans that have a one-piece rear axle, one wheel that's toed-in or toed-out will also induce a steering pull. If toed-in, the wheel will push to the inside. If toed-out, it will pull to the outside. This can also create a dog-tracking problem with both tires suffering toe wear (though the wheel that's off may show more wear).

Caster: Caster is a very important specification since it determines how well your car drives down a straight road. You normally won't get poor tire wear from a bad caster setting, but you will get steering pull to one side. A basic rule of thumb is that the more caster you have, the easier it is to drive in a straight line. A lot of caster gives you greater directional stability.

Caster has no effect on tire wear. Caster is used for vehi-

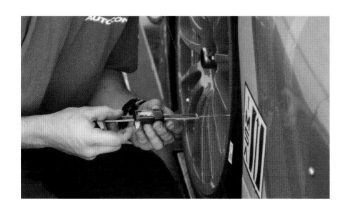

Left: *Now the alignment mechanic can measure from the edge of the wheel to the string. Measurements are taken from both the leading and trailing edge of the wheel. If there is no difference in the distances then the car would have zero toe. If there is a difference then the car has either toe-in or toe-out.* **Right:** *Here we have a 911 with a similar fixture. These fixtures are all custom made to fit a particular car. Obviously they have to be constructed with a high degree of precision.*

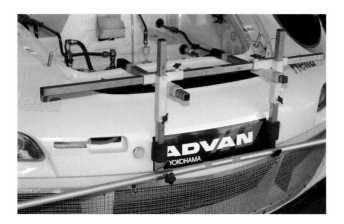

Left: *This is a close-up of the front alignment fixture for a Porsche 911.* **Right:** *Here you can see the string running down the side of the car. Keep in mind that you now have string running down both sides of the car, and they are perfectly parallel with each other. You can understand why some folks call this stringing a car.*

cle stability. Too much caster and the wheels can begin to shimmy like the front wheels on a grocery cart when you go too fast. Too little caster and the wheels don't follow the path well. Typically, caster settings will be from + 1/2 degree to + 4 degrees, but I've seen Mercedes with up to +10 degrees specified. I try to get at least 6 degrees on my Corvette race car.

These higher caster settings give a little more straight-line stability, while lower settings make the steering lighter and the car tend to turn easier. Caster settings that are incorrect by a few degrees from one side of the vehicle to the other usually indicate bent parts.

On many front-wheel-drive vehicles caster is not adjustable. If the caster is out on these cars, it indicates that something is worn or bent, possibly from an accident, and must be repaired or replaced.

Like camber, caster readings should also be set to the preferred specs and be within half a degree side-to-side.

A greater difference side-to-side can make the vehicle pull toward the side with the least caster. Increasing caster increases steering stability while decreasing caster eases steering. Sometimes steering wander can be a problem if the front wheels have insufficient caster.

Adding positive caster to the left front wheel can sometimes compensate steering pull that's caused by road crown. Road crown is how the highway engineers get rid of the rain on the highway. The center of the road is higher than the edge, causing the water to run off the road. It also can raise havoc with your car's ability to stay in a straight line, since the left side of the car is higher than the right side. Road crown is something that no manual discusses. This issue is usually raised by a very experienced, and good, alignment specialist.

If caster is out of range, the shop should check for worn strut or control arm bushings, a dislocated McPherson strut tower, or a bent lower control arm. Keep in mind, too, that caster is not adjustable on a lot of cars.

Camber: The next item you need to be concerned with is camber. Most front-wheel-drive cars have the camber angle set at the factory and the body must be modified or after-market parts installed to change the camber. If no parts are bent, then the body is probably sitting at an angle or too low because of sagging springs. Many times, replacing the springs will bring camber angles right back to factory specifications.

When camber is set to factory specs, the wheels should be more or less perpendicular to the road at normal ride height (a good reason for always checking ride height prior to aligning the wheels). Camber will vary as the suspension travels through jounce and rebound, but as long as the camber changes are the same side-to-side, there should be no problems.

Factory specs often allow for a lot of camber variation. A typical specification may have an acceptable range of up to a full degree of camber either way. If one wheel is at the maximum acceptable limit and the other is at the minimum acceptable limit, you could end up with a difference of almost two full degrees side-to-side. That's way too much camber difference. Consequently, the vehicle will pull toward the front wheel that has the most positive camber or away from the wheel that has the most negative camber. Keeping camber differences to half a degree of less should minimize this kind of problem.

Rear camber is just as important, too. If there's a difference between rear camber alignments, the rear axle can drift to one side or the other, creating a condition similar to rear axle steer that makes the vehicle steer crooked.

So what do you do if the vehicle you're aligning has no factory camber adjustments, or the limited range of adjustment isn't enough to equalize readings or to achieve the preferred settings? Before you install any shims, wedges, offset bushings, or other alignment aids, you should first check to make sure something isn't bent, broken, or worn. A weak or broken spring, a collapsed control arm bushing, a mislocated strut tower or engine cradle, or a bent strut or control arm can all throw camber off the mark.

Checking and comparing steering axis inclination (SAI) readings side-to-side is a good way to identify hidden problems, such as those just described. Even though we tend to think of SAI as a nonadjustable angle that's built into the suspension itself, it is still a useful angle to look at (even if specs are not available) because it can reveal conditions or damage that affect a vehicle's ability to steer straight. On front-wheel-drive cars where the lower control arms are attached to the engine cradle, a shift in the cradle's position to either side will upset SAI

This is a very easy way to adjust the caster on the front of your car. The wishbone is attached to the front axle with chromed clevis pins. These pins are threaded into the wishbone. You can shorten, or lengthen, the upper and lower attachment point length. This will cause the axle to tilt, which is the caster angle. It just can't get much easier.

as well as camber. The result will be a steering lead toward the side with the least SAI. Ideally, right and left SAI readings should be within half a degree of one another.

SOME MORE TERMS

Ride Height

The distance between the frame and the ground is your car's ride height. This can be altered with aftermarket springs (or by cutting the original springs), but altering is not recommended since the entire suspension design of a vehicle is based largely on its original ride height. Also, if ride height varies more than ¼ inch between sides, handling will be compromised and an inspection of the various components should be performed. Sagging springs or a blown-out shock are likely to be the cause.

Track

Track is the distance between the centers of the tires on the same axle. It is basically how wide of a footprint the vehicle has. Using offset wheels, or wheels with a different centerline in relationship to the axle hub, can alter it. A negative offset wheel will increase a vehicle's track while a positive offset wheel will bring the tires closer together. Of course, if you believe the Pontiac ads, "wider is better," you'd want more negative offset for increased stability. But, like all modifications, this can be detrimental if taken too far.

Thrust Angle

You've seen this specification on every alignment printout in the last several decades. You most likely have no clue about what this really means. There's also a good chance the person who handed you the printout had no clue either. Actually, it's real simple.

Thrust angle is the direction that the rear wheels are pointing in relation to the centerline of the vehicle. If the thrust angle is something other than zero, the vehicle will dog track and the steering wheel will not be centered. Think of an imaginary line drawn through the rear axle of your car. This line is at right angles to the rear axle. This line will confirm if the front axle is parallel to the rear axle. It will also confirm if the right and left wheelbases are the same. This may well be the single most important bit of data that is generated by the alignment. This thrust angle should be 0 degrees.

This measurement can only be taken if you have the shop perform a four-wheel alignment. Even if the rear axle is non-adjustable, you need the rear axle readings in order to align the front of the car. Remember that the thrust angle determines the straight-ahead position of the front wheels. A large thrust angle can make a mess of even the most perfectly aligned car. Most often you'll notice that the steering wheel is off center as you drive down the road.

Set Back

Set back is when one front wheel is set farther back than the other wheel. The really good alignment equipment will measure set back and give you a reading in inches or millimeters.

Some manufacturers consider a set back of less than ¼ inch normal tolerance. That's one hell of a lot of set back. When you get beyond that point there's a good chance that something is bent.

SOME MISCELLANEOUS THINGS

In addition to wheel alignment, anything that creates unequal rolling resistance or friction side-to-side on a vehicle's suspension or brakes can make your car steer crooked. This includes things such as under-inflated tires, mismatched tires, or dragging brakes.

Before you check wheel alignment, therefore, always inspect the tires. Check and equalize tire inflation pressures. Note tire sizes and brands. A vehicle will pull toward the side that offers the greatest rolling resistance. So if the tires on both sides of an axle are not the same construction (bias-ply or radial), diameter, tread width, tread pattern, and even

WHY YOUR STEERING PULLS

Three simple conditions must be met for a four-wheeled vehicle to travel in a straight line:
1. All four wheels must be pointing in the same direction. That is, all four wheels must be square to each other and square to the road surface (in other words, parallel to one another, perpendicular to a common centerline, and straight up and down).
2. All four wheels must offer the same amount of rolling resistance. This includes the caster effect between the front wheels that steer.
3. There must be no play in the steering or suspension linkage that positions the wheels.

If all three conditions are not met, your car will drift to one side depending on which forces are at work. This creates a steering pull, which you'll counteract by steering the other way. Having to constantly apply pressure to the steering wheel to keep the car traveling in a straight line can be tiring on a long trip. It can also be hard on the tires.

brand in some instances, there may be enough difference in rolling resistance to induce a slight pull to one side.

A dragging or frozen caliper, or weak or broken return springs, in a drum brake can create enough friction to also cause a noticeable steering pull. If you suspect brake drag, the easiest way to find the offending brake is to raise the wheels off the ground and spin each one by hand.

A vehicle's ability to steer straight can also be undermined if there is excessive play in the steering linkage or wheel bearings. Loose steering tie rod ends, idler arms, a worn steering rack, even loose rack mounts can all have an influence on directional stability. Be sure to perform a thorough inspection of the steering and suspension before aligning the wheels.

The alignment of the steering linkage itself is also important. If the rack, center link, and/or steering arms are not parallel to the ground, it may create unequal toe changes that result in a bump steer condition when the suspension travels through jounce and rebound. Measuring and comparing the height of the inner and outer tie rod ends on each side can help you identify this kind of problem. Another technique is to check for equal toe changes on each side when the suspension is raised and then lowered.

Another condition that may even cause a vehicle to steer crooked is a power steering problem. Internal leaks in the power steering control valve can route pressure to where it isn't needed. The pressure imbalance may make the car drift to one side or, if bad enough, the car may try to steer itself with no assistance

GLOSSARY

Adhesion This refers to a static situation, and how sticky a tire is. If we're talking about sticking in a dynamic situation, it's generally called traction.

Aspect Ratio This is simply the ratio between the width of the tire and the height of the tire's sidewall. It has nothing to do with the width of the tread on the tire. Let's take a 40 series tire as an example. This means that the height of the sidewall is 40 percent of the width of the tire.

Asymmetric Tread This is a case where the left side of the tire tread is different from the right side; you actually have an inner edge and an outer edge. This is used to enhance the performance of the tire. Tires can use one side for things such as dispersing water, while the other side can be made to handle cornering stress. Either way you're screwed if you want to rotate these tires. Even worse is when the front and back tires are different sizes. This will usually become a very expensive set of tires to replace.

Backspacing The distance from where the hub pad surface is to the rear edge of the wheel.

Bead This is the reinforced component of the tire that's located on the inner edge of the diameter on both the inner and outer edges of the tire. This is what contacts the wheel. As you put air in the tire, the bead is forced on to the wheel and a seal is created.

Bead Seat This is the part of the wheel where the tire bead seats. It's the inner lip and must be absolutely clean when you mount the tires.

Bias-Belted Construction This construction is similar to bias ply but with the addition of two or more belts under the tread in an effort to stabilize and strengthen the tread. These belts improve tread life by reducing any tread movement during contact with the road.

Bias-Ply Construction This type of construction has two to four layers of ply cord that run diagonally from the bead to the tread.

Blister Blisters form from excessive heat. Think of it as an air bubble on the side wall or tread. It's not uncommon on racing tires.

Blocks Blocks are defined by the placement of grooves in the tread. The face of the block actually makes direct contact with the road surface as the tire rotates. One problem with tread blocks is that they wear unevenly, which can cause substantial noise issues.

Beadlocks A device that captures the tire bead between its flanges and is generally secured by bolts. The goal is to keep the tire bead from dismounting. They're usually used in dirt, circle-track, or off-road applications where low tire pressures are used and hitting ruts or other vehicles is common. The inner ring may be welded onto a standard wheel increasing wheel width by anywhere from 1 1/2 to 2 inches. The inner ring may be formed as part of the wheel when the wheel is made in the factory. The outer ring is then bolted onto the inner ring with the bead clamped between them. Anywhere between 16 and 32 bolts at around 10 lb-ft are used around the circumference of the wheel to keep the clamp tight. The rings and bolts can cause problems with balancing the wheel and tire because all the added weight is on one side. It's important to note that most standard beadlocks clamp only the outside bead. This is fine in most cases because the outside bead is the side that comes unseated most often while off-roading.

Bolt Circle This is the diameter of an imaginary circle that runs through the centers of the wheel mounting bolts. It's usually expressed in inches such as 4.75'.

Bolt Pattern Bolt patterns can be four-,five-, six-, or eight-lug holes. A bolt circle of 4x100 would indicate a 4 lug pattern on a circle with a diameter of 100mm.

Burnouts When drag racers approach the starting line, (also known as the staging area), they apply water (formerly bleach) to the driven tires either by backing into a small puddle (called the water box) or by having it sprayed on. The car then exits the water and does a burnout to heat the tires, making them even stickier. Some cars have a "line-lock," which prevents the rear brakes from engaging when the brake pedal is depressed (this line-lock can be toggled on and off). This allows the car to remain stationary, with only the front brakes applied. Cars in street-legal classes are the only exception to this pre-race burnout ritual, as the grooves street tires tend to retain some of the water in the tread.

Caster When you turn the steering wheel, the front wheels respond by turning on a pivot attached to the suspension system. Caster is the angle of this steering pivot and is measured in degrees from the side of the vehicle. If the top of the pivot is leaning toward the rear of the car, then the caster is positive. If the top of the pivot is leaning toward the front, caster is negative. If the caster is out of adjustment, it can cause problems in straight-line tracking. If the caster is different from side to side, the vehicle will pull to the side with the less positive caster. If the caster is equal but too negative all around, the steering will be light and the vehicle will wander and be difficult to keep in a straight line. If the caster is equal on all wheels but too positive, the steering will be heavy and the steering wheel may kick when you hit a bump. Caster has little affect on tire wear. The best way to visualize caster is to picture a shopping cart caster. The pivot of this type of caster, while not at an angle, intersects the ground ahead of the wheel contact patch. When the wheel is behind the pivot at the point where it contacts the ground, it is in positive caster. Picture yourself trying to push the cart and keep the wheel ahead of the pivot. The wheel will continually try to turn from straight ahead, which is what happens when a car has very little caster angle. Caster, like camber, isn't adjustable on a lot of front-wheel-drive vehicles. If the caster is out on these cars, it indicates that something is worn or bent, possibly from an accident, and must be repaired or replaced.

Center Bore This is large hole in the middle of the wheel. In a hub-centric mounting system this is machined space to provide a very precise fit to the hub of the car. With lug-centric mounting systems the center bore is generally designed to fit a variety of vehicles.

Contact Patch This is simply the area of the tire tread that touches the surface of the road. The shape of a tire's contact patch, or footprint, greatly influences its performance and is dependent on its profile or aspect ratio. Low-profile tires (most performance tires) have a short and wide contact patch that is effective in converting the driver's input into very responsive handling, cornering stability, and traction—especially on dry roads. High-profile tires (light truck and most passenger tires) have a long and narrow contact patch that helps to provide predictable handling, a smooth ride, and especially good

traction in snow.

Cross Section The maximum distance between the exterior sidewalls when the tire is inflated.

Crown The center area of the tire's footprint.

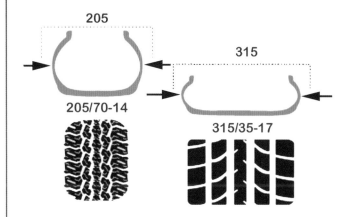

Flat Lug Seat A type of lug nut or bolt that presses directly against the wheel. There is no cone shape or angle.

Gravity Casting This is the most common, and cheapest, method for producing alloy wheels. The molten aluminum uses only gravity to fill the mold. These wheels are extremely weak and often will be very heavy to make up for lack of strength.

Streetlocks Some people want their trucks to look as if it has beadlocks without actually paying for real beadlocks. Many wheels are therefore made to look like beadlocks but they don't actually lock anything. The off-road community generally refers to these as streetlocks since the owners typically don't use them for off-road use.

Tire Pressure This is the force created by compressed air (or nitrogen) inside the tire. It can be expressed in pounds per square inch (psi) or Bar, which is actually kilograms (Kgs) per square inch.

Tread Void This refers to the channels, or grooves, in the tire that force water away from the tread contact area.

APPENDIX I
TIRE INTERCHANGE CHART

NUMERIC "90-" to "80"-series		ALPHA NUMERIC* 78- to 50-series	EURO-METRIC "82"-series	P-METRIC 80-, 75 -series	EURO-METRIC or P-METRIC 70-series	65-series	60-series	50-series
5.20-10			145R10		165/70R10			
5.20-12			145R12	P145/80R12	165/70R12			
5.60-12	6.00-12		155R12	P155/80R12				
						165/65R13		
			145R13					
			155R13	P155/80R13	175/70R13		195/60R13	215/50R13
5.60-13	6.00-13	A	165R13	P165/80R13	185/70R13		205/60R13	
	6.50-13	B	175R13	P175/80R13				
		C		P185/80R13				
	7.00-13	D	185R13					
			195R13					
5.60-14	6.00-14		145R14			175/65R14		
6.00-14	6.45-14		155R14		175/70R14	185/65R14		
		B	165R14	P175/75R14	185/70R14	195/65R14	205/60R14	
6.50-14	6.95-14	C	175R14	P185/75R14	195/70R14		215/60R14	
		D						
7.00-14	7.35-14	E	185R14	P195/75R14	205/70R14		225/60R14	245/50R14
7.50-14	7.75-14	F	195R14	P205/75R14	215/70R14		235/60R14	
8.00-14	8.25-14	G	205R14	P215/75R14	225/70R14		245/60R14	265/50R14
8.50-14	8.55-14	H	215R14	P225/75R14				
9.00-14		J	225R14					
9.50-14		L						
	5.60-15	A	155R15	P155/80R15		185/65R15	195/60R15	
6.00-15		B	165R15	P165/80R15	185/70R15	195/65R15	205/60R15	225/50R15
6.50-15	6.85-15	C	175R15		195/70R15	205/65R15	215/60R15	
		D						
	7.35-15	E	185R15	P195/75R15	205/70R15	215/65R15	225/60R15	
6.70-15	7.75-15	F	195R15	P205/75R15	215/70R15		235/60R15	
	8.15-15							
7.10-15		G	205R15	P215/75R15	225/70R15	235/65R15	245/60R15	265/50R15
	8.25-15							
	8.45-15							
7.60-15		H	215R15	P225/75R15	235/70R15		255/60R15	275/50R15
	8.55-15							
8.00-15	8.85-15	J	225R15	P225/75R15	235/70R15		265/60R15	
8.20-15	9.00-15	K						
	9.15-15	L	235R15	P235/75R15	255/70R15		275/60R15	295/50R15
		N						

*When you replace Alpha Numeric tires with Euro-metric or P-metric tires, look for the Euro-metric or P-metric size listed in the equivalent aspect ratio. For example, when replacing an FR78-14, you would look up the appropriate 75-series size, the 205/75R/14. If replacing an FR70-14, you would look up the appropriate 70-series size, the 215/70R/14. If replacing an FR60-14, you would look up the appropriate 60-series size, the 235/60R/14.

This chart doesn't imply complete interchangeability. It's simply a guide, a starting point. The next step is checking the actual dimensions. When changing tire sizes, dimensional clearances must be checked.

APPENDIX II
WHEEL LUG NUT AND
BOLT TORQUE
SPECIFICATIONS

Make/Model	Year	Torque
Acura		
All models	1990-05	80 lb-ft
Alfa Romeo		
All models	1991-95	75 lb-ft
Aston Martin		
Vanquish	2002-05	95 lb-ft
All other models	1983-05	75 lb-ft
Audi		
All models	1982-05	90 lb-ft
Bentley		
Arnage	2002-04	100 lb-ft
Arnage	1999-01	75 lb-ft
Azure/LeMans	2001-02	85 lb-ft
Continental GT	2003-05	110 lb-ft
All other models	1989-05	50 lb-ft
BMW/Mini		
745 & 760	2002-05	100 lb-ft
Mini Cooper	2002-05	105 lb-ft
All other models	1982-05	90 lb-ft
Buick		
All models	1982-05	100 lb-ft
Cadillac		
Catera	1997-01	80 lb-ft
Deville HD Spec.	1997-01	140 lb-ft
All other models	1977-05	100 lb-ft
Chevrolet / Geo		
Aveo	2004-05	90 lb-ft
Metro	1991-99	50 lb-ft
Prizm	1989-02	80 lb-ft
Storm	1990-93	85 lb-ft
All other models	1987-05	100 lb-ft
Chrysler		
Cirrus	1995-00	100 lb-ft
Concorde	1993-04	110 lb-ft
Crossfire	2004-05	85 lb-ft
Fifth Avenue (RWD)	1983-90	85 lb-ft
LeBaron/New Yorker	1984-96	95 lb-ft
LHS/300M/300C/300	1999-05	110 lb-ft
LHS	1994-97	95 lb-ft
PT Cruiser	2001-05	110 lb-ft
Prowler Roadster	2002	100 lb-ft
Sebring Conv.	1996-05	105 lb-ft
Sebring Coupe	1999-05	80 lb-ft
Sebring Coupe	1996-98	100 lb-ft
Sebring Sedan	2001-05	110 lb-ft
T/C by Maserati	1989-91	95 lb-ft
Daewoo		
Lanos/Nubria	1999-03	90 lb-ft
Leganza	1999-03	80 lb-ft
Dodge		
Avenger	1999-00	80 lb-ft
Avenger	1995-98	100 lb-ft
Charger	2006	110 lb-ft
Colt	1976-94	80 lb-ft
Daytona/Dynasty	1984-93	95 lb-ft
Intrepid	1999-04	110 lb-ft
Intrepid	1993-98	95 lb-ft
Magnum	2005-06	110 lb-ft
Neon	2000-05	110 lb-ft
Neon	1999	100 lb-ft
Neon	1995-98	95 lb-ft
Omni	1984-90	95 lb-ft
Shadow	1987-94	95 lb-ft
Spirit	1989-94	95 lb-ft
Stealth	1991-96	100 lb-ft
Stratus	1995-99	100 lb-ft
Stratus Coupe	2001-05	80 lb-ft
Stratus Sedan	2000-05	110 lb-ft
Viper	1993-04	100 lb-ft
Vista	1984-91	60 lb-ft
Eagle		
Premier & Monaco*	1989-92	75 lb-ft
*With aluminum wheels		100 lb-ft
Medallion	1988	65 lb-ft
Summit	1989-96	80 lb-ft
Talon	1990-98	100 lb-ft
Vison	1993-97	95 lb-ft
Ferrari		
360 Modena	2000-05	80 lb-ft
550/575 Maranello	1998-05	100 lb-ft

456 M GT/GTA	1995-04	90 lb-ft
Testarossa(5 bolts)	1988-91	75 lb-ft
348/Mondial T	1989-94	75 lb-ft
All other models		90 lb-ft

Ford

Aspire	1994-97	85 lb-ft
Contour	1999-00	95 lb-ft
Contour	1998	85 lb-ft
Contour	1995-97	65 lb-ft
Crown Victoria	2000-05	100 lb-ft
Escort/ZX2	1991-04	85 lb-ft
Escort/EXP	1981-90	100 lb-ft
Festiva	1988-93	85 lb-ft
Five Hundred	2005	100 lb-ft
Focus	2000-05	95 lb-ft
Freestyle	2005	100 lb-ft
Mustang	1979-05	100 lb-ft
Probe	1989-97	85 lb-ft
Taurus	2000-05	95 lb-ft
Taurus	1986-96	100 lb-ft
Tempo	1984-96	100 lb-ft
Thunderbird	1975-05	100 lb-ft
All other models	1984-99	100 lb-ft

Honda

All models	1984-04	80 lb-ft

Hyundai

All models	1986-05	80 lb-ft

Infiniti

G20	1999-02	100 lb-ft
All other models	1990-05	85 lb-ft

Isuzu

All models	1983-93	85 lb-ft

Jaguar

S Type	2000-05	95 lb-ft
All other models	1989-05	75 lb-ft

Kia

All models	1993-05	85 lb-ft

Lamborghini

All models	1990-04	80 lb-ft

Lexus

All models	1990-05	75 lb-ft

Lincoln

All models	1984-05	100 lb-ft

Maserati

Spider	2002-04	90 lb-ft
All other models	1989-91	75 lb-ft

Mazda

Millenia	1995-02	90 lb-ft
All other models	1976-05	85 lb-ft

Mercedes

Models with 14mm bolts	1994-05	110 lb-ft
All other models	1994-05	80 lb-ft

Mercury

Capri	1991-94	90 lb-ft
Cougar	1999-02	95 lb-ft
Grand Marquis	2000-04	100 lb-ft
Marauder	2003-04	95 lb-ft
Montego	2005	100 lb-ft
Mystique	1999-00	95 lb-ft
Mystique	1998	85 lb-ft
Mystique	1995-97	65 lb-ft
Sable	2000-04	95 lb-ft
Sable	1995-99	100 lb-ft
Tracer	1988-99	90 lb-ft
All other models	1984-05	100 lb-ft

Merkur

Scorpio	1988-90	70 lb-ft
XR4Ti	1985-89	100 lb-ft

Mitsubishi

3000 GT	1991-99	100 lb-ft
Eclipse	1990-99	100 lb-ft
Lancer	2002-04	80 lb-ft
Precis*	1987-94	60 lb-ft
* With aluminum wheels		70 lb-ft
All other models	1987-05	80 lb-ft

Nissan

Sentra/Sentra E	1990-95	75 lb-ft
All other models	1987-05	90 lb-ft

Oldsmobile

All models	1977-04	100 lb-ft

Panoz

All models	1999-05	90 lb-ft

Plymouth

Acclaim/Reliant	1989-95	95 lb-ft
Breeze	2000	105 lb-ft
Breeze	1999	100 lb-ft
Breeze	1996-98	95 lb-ft
Colt	1983-94	80 lb-ft
Grand Fury	1980-89	85 lb-ft
Horizon	1978-90	95 lb-ft
Laser	1990-94	95 lb-ft
Neon (see Dodge)		
Prowler	2000-01	100 lb-ft
Sundance	1987-94	95 lb-ft
Turismo	1982-87	95 lb-ft
Vista*	1984-94	55 lb-ft
* With aluminum wheels		80 lb-ft

Pontiac

LeMans	1989-93	65 lb-ft
Vibe	2003-05	75 lb-ft
All other models	1990-05	100 lb-ft

Porsche

Carrera GT	2004-05	407 lb-ft
All other models	1972-05	95 lb-ft

Rolls Royce

Parkwood/Seraph	1997-02	75 lb-ft
Phantom	2004-05	105 lb-ft
All other models	1989-02	50 lb-ft

Saab

9-2X	2005	75 lb-ft
9-3 / 9-5	1999-05	80 lb-ft
900 models*	1995-98	80 lb-ft
*With aluminum wheels		85 lb-ft
9000 models	1994-98	90 lb-ft
All other models	1988-93	90 lb-ft
All other models	1976-87	80 lb-ft

Saturn

EV-1 Electric	1997-02	100 lb-ft
L Series	2003-04	80 lb-ft
L Series	2000-02	95 lb-ft
Vue	2002-04	100 lb-ft
All other models	1991-05	100 lb-ft

Scion

All Models	2004-05	75 lb-ft

Subaru

SVX	1992-97	90 lb-ft
All other models	1985-05	75 lb-ft

Suzuki

Aerio	2002-05	65 lb-ft
Esteem	1996-02	65 lb-ft
Forenza	2004-05	90 lb-ft
Reno	2005	65 lb-ft
Swift	1989-01	50 lb-ft
Verona	2004-05	80 lb-ft
X-90	1996-98	70 lb-ft

Toyota

All models	1985-05	80 lb-ft

Volkswagen

All models	1999-05	90 lb-ft
All models	1988-98	80 lb-ft

Volvo

S / V40	2000-05	80 lb-ft
S 60	2001-05	100 lb-ft
C70 / S70	1998-04	80 lb-ft
S 80	1999-05	100 lb-ft
V 70	1998-05	100 lb-ft
200 Series	1981-93	85 lb-ft
700/900, S90/V90	1983-98	65 lb-ft
850 Series	1993-97	80 lb-ft

Mini Vans, Light Trucks, and SUVs

Make/Model	Year	Torque
Acura		
MDX	2001-05	80 lb-ft
SLX	1996-99	90 lb-ft
BMW		
X5	2000-05	105 lb-ft
X3	2004-05	85 lb-ft
Buick		
Rendezvous	2002-05	100 lb-ft
Cadillac		
Escalade / EXT	1999-05	140 lb-ft
SRX	2004-05	95 lb-ft
Chevrolet / GMC		
Astro/Safari Van	1985-05	100 lb-ft
Avalanche	2002-05	140 lb-ft
C/K Blazer/Suburban/ Jimmy (full size)	1992-95	120 lb-ft
C/K Pickup (Full) (SRW/DRW)	1996-00	140 lb-ft
C30 HD (DRW) 5/8-18	1996-00	175 lb-ft
C/K Pickup	1988-95	120 lb-ft
C/K Pickup (DRW)	1988-95	140 lb-ft
Colorado/Canyon	2004-05	100 lb-ft
Denali	1997-05	140 lb-ft
Envoy/XUV	1998-05	100 lb-ft
Equinox	2004-05	100 lb-ft
Express/Savana	1996-05	140 lb-ft
G10/G15, G20/G25, G30/ G35(SRW/DRW)	1996-99	140 lb-ft
G10/G15, G20/G25, (Full Size)	1988-95	100 lb-ft
G30/G35 Full Size	1988-95	120 lb-ft
G30/G35 (DRW) (Full Size)	1988-95	140 lb-ft
Lumina APV	1990-93	100 lb-ft
Lumina Minivan	1994-96	100 lb-ft
R10/R15-Full Size Suburban/Blazer	1989-91	100 lb-ft
R20/R25,R30/R35-Full Size Suburban (SRW)	1989-91	120 lb-ft
SSR	2003-05	80 lb-ft
Suburban (DRW)	1989-91	125 lb-ft
S/T Pickup/Blazer/Trail Blazer/Jimmy	1992-05	100 lb-ft
S10/S15 Pickup/Blazer/ Jimmy	1982-92	80 lb-ft
Silverado/Sierra	1999-05	140 lb-ft
Silverado/Sierra HD (DRW) 5/8-18	1999-05	175 lb-ft
Suburban/Tahoe/Yukon	1996-05	140 lb-ft
Tracker	1990-99	60 lb-ft
Tracker	2000-05	70 lb-ft
T10/T15 Pickup/Blazer/ Jimmy	1982-91	100 lb-ft
V10/V15 Full Size Suburban Suburban/Blazer	1990-91	100 lb-ft

w/ Aluminum Wheels	1988-89	100 lb-ft
w/ Steel Wheels	1988-89	90 lb-ft
V20/V25,V30/V35 Full Size		
Suburban (SRW)	1989-91	120 lb-ft
Suburban (DRW)	1989-91	125 lb-ft
Uplander	2005	100 lb-ft
Venture Minivan	1997-04	100 lb-ft

Chrysler

Pacifica	2004-05	85 lb-ft
PT Cruiser	2001-05	110 lb-ft
Town & Country	2000-05	110 lb-ft
Town & Country	1999	100 lb-ft
Town & Country	1990-98	95 lb-ft
Voyager	2001-03	110 lb-ft

Diahatsu

Rocky (All)	1990-92	85 lb-ft

Dodge

Grand Caravan/Caravan	2000 05	110 lb ft
Grand Caravan/Caravan	1999	100 lb-ft
Dakota Pickup (All)	1985-98	95 lb-ft
Dakota Pickup	1994-05	110 lb-ft
Durango	1998-05	110 lb-ft
Pickup (D&W series)		
D100/150,D200/250	1972-93	105 lb-ft
D300/350(1/2' stud)	1979-93	105 lb-ft
D300/350(5/8' stud)	1979-93	105 lb-ft
w/ flanged 5/8' stud	1979-93	200 lb-ft
Ramcharger	1979-93	350 lb-ft
Rampage (FWD)	1979-93	105 lb-ft
Ram 50 Pickup	1982-84	90 lb-ft
Ram Pickup	1987-93	100 lb-ft
1500	1994-01	110 lb-ft
1500	2002-05	135 lb-ft
2500	1994-01	150 lb-ft
2500	2002-05	135 lb-ft
3500	1994-01	160 lb-ft
3500	2002-05	145 lb-ft
SRT-10	2004-05	135 lb-ft
Ram Van		
B1500	2002-05	110 lb-ft
B1500	1998-01	115 lb-ft
B1500	1995-97	110 lb-ft
B2500 (9/16"-18 studs)	1999-05	150 lb-ft
B2500	1998	115 lb-ft
B2500	1997	110 lb-ft
B3500 (9/16"-18 studs)	1999-05	150 lb-ft
B3500 w/out 5/8" studs	1995-98	115 lb-ft
with 5/8" studs	1995-98	225 lb-ft
B150	1994	110 lb-ft
B250/350 w/out 5/8" studs	1994	115 lb-ft
with 5/8" studs	1994	225 lb-ft
Ram Van (FWD)	1984-93	95 lb-ft
Ram Wagon		
B1500	2002	110 lb-ft
B1500	1998-01	115 lb-ft
B1500	1995-97	110 lb-ft
B2500 (9/16"-18 studs)	1992-02	150 lb-ft
B2500	1998	115 lb-ft
B2500	1997	110 lb-ft
B2500	1995-96	115 lb-ft
B3500 (9/16'-18 studs)	1999-02	150 lb-ft
B3500 w/out 5/58' studs	1995-98	115 lb-ft
with 5/8' stud	1995-98	225 lb-ft
B150	1994	110 lb-ft
B250/B350 w/out 5/8" studs	1994	115 lb-ft
with 5/8" studs	1994	225 lb-ft
Ram Wagon		
B100/150	1972-93	105 lb-ft
B200/250	1972-93	105 lb-ft
B300/350 (1/2' studs)	1979-93	105 lb-ft
B300/350 (5/8'studs)	1979-93	200 lb-ft
w/ flanged 5/8' studs	1979-93	350 lb-ft
Sprinter 2500	2004-05	140 lb-ft
Sprinter 3500	2004-05	180 lb-ft

Ford

Aerostar	1986-97	100 lb-ft
Bronco	1987-96	100 lb-ft
Bronco II	1987-90	100 lb-ft
Escape	2001-05	100 lb-ft
Excursion All	2001-05	160 lb-ft
Excursion	2000	150 lb-ft
Expedition (12mm stud)	1997-00	*100 lb-ft
Expedition (14mm stud)	2000-05	*150 lb-ft
Explorer	1991-05	100 lb-ft
E150	1975-05	100 lb-ft
E250/350 (8 lug 9/16'-18)	1988-05	140 lb-ft
E Super Duty (10 lug)	2002-05	165 lb-ft
F150 (12mm stud)	1988-00	*100 lb-ft
F150 (14mm stud)	2000-05	*150 lb-ft
F250/350 (8 lug 9/16'-18)	2001-03	160 lb-ft
F250/350 (8 lug 9/16'-18)	1999-00	150 lb-ft
F250/350 (8 lug 9/16'-18)	1988-98	140 lb-ft
F Super Duty		
(10 lug 9/16'-18)	1999-05	165 lb-ft
(10 lug 9/16'-18)	1996-98	140 lb-ft
Ranger Pickup	1987-05	100 lb-ft
Windstar/Freestar	1995-05	100 lb-ft

For 2000 model year, check lug nut washer for correct torque setting.

Honda

CR-V	1997-05	80 lb-ft
Element	2003-05	80 lb-ft
Odyssey	1995-05	80 lb-ft
Passport	1994-02	90 lb-ft
Pilot	2003-05	80 lb-ft
Ridgeline	2005-06	100 lb-ft

Hummer

H1/H2	2003-05	140 lb-ft

Hyundai

Santa Fe	2001-05	80 lb-ft

Infinity

FX35/FX45	2003-05	80 lb-ft
QX4	1997-05	105 lb-ft

Isuzu

Ascender	2003-05	80 lb-ft
Amigo	1992-94	**85 lb-ft
Amigo	1991	*75 lb-ft
Axiom	2002-04	95 lb-ft
Hombre	1996-00	95 lb-ft
Oasis	1996-99	80 lb-ft
Pickup	1995	**85 lb-ft
Pickup	1991	*75 lb-ft
Pickup	1990	**85 lb-ft
Rodeo	1991-04	*65 lb-ft
Trooper	1984-02	85 lb-ft
Vehicross	1999-01	85 lb-ft
* with aluminum wheels		85 lb-ft
** with aluminum wheels		95 lb-ft

Jeep

Cherokee	1994-01	110 lb-ft
Comanche	1984-92	75 lb-ft
Grand Cherokee	1993-05	110 lb-ft
Liberty	2002-05	110 lb-ft
Wagoneer 5-lug		110 lb-ft
Wagoneer 6-lug		75 lb-ft
Wrangler	1994-05	110 lb-ft
Wrangler/CJ	1990-93	80 lb-ft

Kia

Sedona	2002-04	75 lb-ft
Sorento	2003-04	85 lb-ft
Sportage	1995-05	85 lb-ft

Land Rover

Defender 90/110	1993-97	95 lb-ft
Discovery	1994-99	95 lb-ft
Discovery Series II	1999-05	105 lb-ft
Freelander S/SE/HSE	2002-05	85 lb-ft
LR3	2005	100 lb-ft
Ranger Rover Classic	1987-95	95 lb-ft
Ranger Rover HSE	1996-02	85 lb-ft
Ranger Rover HSE	2003-05	105 lb-ft
Range Rover SE	1995-01	85 lb-ft

Lexus

GX470	2003-05	85 lb-ft
LX450	1996-97	80 lb-ft
LX470	1998-05	95 lb-ft
RX300/330	1999-05	80 lb-ft

Lincoln

Aviator	2003-05	100 lb-ft
Blackwood	2002-04	155 lb-ft
Navigator (12mm stud)	1998-00	*100 lb-ft
Navigator (14mm stud)	2000-04	*150 lb-ft
Mark LT	2006	150 lb-ft

For 2000 model year, check lug nut washer for correct torque setting.

Mazda

B2200	1986-93	*85 lb-ft
B2300/B4000	1994-05	100 lb-ft
B2500/3000	1998-05	100 lb-ft
B2600	1987-93	*85 lb-ft
MPV	1996-05	85 lb-ft
Navaho	1991-94	100 lb-ft
Tribute	2001-05	105 lb-ft
*with Chrome Steel Wheels		100 lb-ft

Mercedes

M-class	1998-05	110 lb-ft

Mercury

Mountaineer	1997-05	100 lb-ft
Villager	1993-02	80 lb-ft

Mitsubishi

Endeavor	2004-05	80 lb-ft
Montero	2000-04	85 lb-ft
Montero	1999	100 lb-ft
Montero	1997-98	110 lb-ft
Montero	1994-96	85 lb-ft
Montero	1993	100 lb-ft
Montero Sport	2000-05	85 lb-ft
Montero Sport	1999	100 lb-ft
Montero Sport	1997-98	105 lb-ft
Outlander	2003-05	80 lb-ft
Pickups	1992-96	100 lb-ft
Pickups	1989-91	85 lb-ft
Van/Wagons	1989-90	100 lb-ft

Nissan

Pathfinder/Frontier	1987-05	105 lb-ft
Pickups	1987-97	105 lb-ft
Pickups (DRW)	1987-91	200 lb-ft
Quest	1995-05	85 lb-ft
Titan	2004-05	105 lb-ft
Xterra/Murano	2000-05	80 lb-ft

Oldsmobile

Bravada	1991-04	100 lb-ft
Silouette	1990-04	100 lb-ft

Plymouth

Voyager/Grand Voyager	2000	110 lb-ft
Voyager/Grand Voyager	1999	100 lb-ft
Voyager/Grand Voyager	1984-98	95 lb-ft

Pontiac

Aztec	2001-05	100 lb-ft
Montana/Trans Sport	1990-05	100 lb-ft

Saturn

Vue	2002-05	100 lb-ft

Subaru

Baja	2003-05	75 lb-ft
Forester	1998-05	75 lb-ft

Suzuki

Grand Vitara/Vitara	1999-05	70 lb-ft
Samuri	1991-94	80 lb-ft
Samuri	1985-90	55 lb-ft
Sidekick	1989-98	75 lb-ft
X-90	1996-98	70 lb-ft

Toyota

Highlander	2001-05	80 lb-ft
Land Cruiser	1999-05	100 lb-ft
Land Cruiser	1994-98	*105 lb-ft
Land Cruiser	1989-93	115 lb-ft
Pickup 2WD (SRW)	1989-94	100 lb-ft
Pickup 2WD (DRW)	1989-94	170 lb-ft
Pickup 4WD	1991-92	80 lb-ft
Previa/Rav4/Sienna	1991-05	80 lb-ft
Sequoia	2001-05	85 lb-ft
Tacoma	1999-05	85 lb-ft
Tacoma	1995-98	80 lb-ft
Tundra	2000-05	85 lb-ft
T100	1995-98	80 lb-ft
4 Runner	1999-05	85 lb-ft
4 Runner	1988-98	80 lb-ft
* With aluminum wheels		80 lb-ft

Volkswagen

EuroVan	1997-03	130 lb-ft
EuroVan	1992-96	115 lb-ft
Pickups	1979-84	80 lb-ft
Touareg	2004-05	120 lb-ft

Volvo

XC90	2003-05	105 lb-ft

Motorhomes & Box Vans with Double Cap Lug Nuts

With 5/8' studs	450 lb-ft

Trailers & Applications Not Listed

7/16-inch studs	80 lb-ft
1/2-inch studs	100 lb-ft
9/16-inch studs	140 lb-ft
5/8-inch studs	175 lb-ft
10mm studs	50 lb-ft
12mm studs	100 lb-ft
14mm studs	120 lb-ft

Abbreviation Key:
RWD - Rear Wheel Drive
FWD - Front Wheel Drive
SRW - Single Wheel Drive
DRW - Dual Wheel Drive
2WD - Two Wheel Drive
4WD - Four Wheel Drive

INDEX

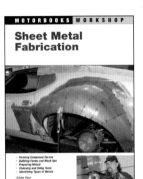
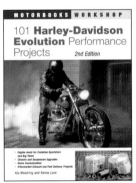

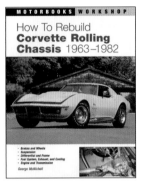
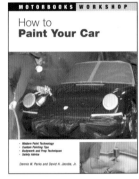